We spend so much of our lives learning how to be accepted that we forget how to be real. This book is an invitation to remember. Through her own story, Alexis illuminates a struggle that feels profoundly universal: the tension between belonging and becoming, between performance and truth. Compassionate, insightful and practical *Real* is ultimately a reminder that beneath the roles we play and the masks we wear, there remains something worth returning to — our shared humanity.

—Dr Dale Whelehan,
Asst Professor Psychology, Trinity College Dublin;
TIME Magazine 100 Most Influential People
in the World (Health), 2024; *Forbes* 30
Under 30 Europe, 2024

This thoughtful book will help you understand how modern technologies like social media and AI amplify the dark side of individualism, thereby diluting the original value of authenticity and the quest to discover who we are: one of the best articulations of the perils of misunderstanding that the right to be you should very rarely override your obligation to others, and that we are far better off seeking to be our best than our unfiltered or 'real' self, especially in high-stakes situations.

—Tomas Chamorro-Premuzic,
Professor of Business Psychology at Columbia and UCL and
Chief Science Officer at Russell Reynolds

Alexis Zahner brings a practical, rigorous approach—and her own honest reckoning—to a problem most of us are living, but few of us address: how social media is quietly eroding our sense of self. *Real* is both a clear-eyed explanation of what's happening and a hands-on guide for reclaiming the identity, presence, and connections that get lost in the scroll. This book helps you understand yourself well enough that your relationship with technology stops undermining your relationship with everything that matters.

—Amy Gallo,
author of *Getting Along: How to Work with Anyone (Even Difficult People)* and
contributing editor at *Harvard Business Review*

Social media does not just compete for our attention; it rewrites our ambitions. *Real* is a clear-eyed guide to letting go of borrowed ambitions and reclaiming the agency to build a life of our own.

—Anne-Laure Le Cunff
author of *Tiny Experiments*

The most widespread addiction today is social media addiction, and its peculiar predicament is that you can't simply quit the habit—social media are an integral part of both personal and professional life. Alexis Zahner's account of her struggles with this conundrum provides concrete advice on how to live more productively with social media as well as a highly relatable existential exploration of selfhood. Readers won't regret trading some of the time they commonly spend on Instagram or TikTok for reading this book.

—Dr Hans-Georg Moeller,

Professor, Department of Philosophy and Religious Studies, University of Macau; bestselling author of *Genuine Pretending* and *Your and Your Profile Self;* creator of the popular YouTube channel Carefree Wandering

This is the ideal handbook for building a healthier relationship with technology. Deeply researched, thought-provoking, witty and wise, *Real* provides a template for a life with true meaning. It's practical, positive, and future-focused. Highly recommended!

—Tracey Spicer AM,

Walkey Award-winning journalist, newsreader and author of *Man Made: How the bias of the past is being built into the future*

real

real

Reconnecting to Yourself in a World of Likes and Lies

Alexis Zahner

WILEY

First published 2027 by John Wiley & Sons Australia, Ltd

ISBN: 978-1-394-44569-1

NATIONAL LIBRARY OF AUSTRALIA

A catalogue record for this book is available from the National Library of Australia

Registered Office
John Wiley & Sons Australia, Ltd. Level 4, 600 Bourke Street, Melbourne, VIC 3000, Australia

For details of our global editorial offices, customer services, and more information about Wiley products visit us at www.wiley.com.

Wiley also publishes its books in a variety of electronic formats and by print-on-demand. Some content that appears in standard print versions of this book may not be available in other formats.

Cover design by Wiley
Cover Images: Shanina/Getty Images, Prostock-studio/Shutterstock, Irina Bg/Shutterstock, Artmim/Shutterstock, PeopleImages/Shutterstock

Set in 12/16.5pt and Adobe Garamond Pro by Straive, Chennai, India.

Printed and bound by CPI Group (UK) Ltd, Croydon, CR0 4YY

C9781394445691_040926

The manufacturer's authorized representative according to the EU General Product Safety Regulation is Wiley-VCH GmbH, Boschstr. 12, 69469 Weinheim, Germany, e-mail: Product_Safety@wiley.com.

Contents

RIP: In loving memory of Alexis Zahner

Uninspiringly average amateur athlete, meme curator and self-proclaimed 'thought leader'

1991–TBD (her battery died mid procrastination doomscroll)

Alexis succumbed to the algorithm, buried beneath a landslide of sponsored content, fake DMs, influencer-recommended life hacks and a final post that only got 39 likes (on a *Sunday*, no less).

Known to her followers as @alexis_laine_zahner surfer-emoji sun-emoji #doingless (after three personal aesthetic rebrands), she was a maverick for a carefully under-edited but very much curated 'candid' shot. With an ability to filter a selfie more naturally than most could filter their drinking water, her captions were understated yet profound, much like a modern-day Buddha—if the Buddha had written in all lowercase with flaming heart emojis for emphasis.

A pioneer of the 'soft launch' era, she once strategically debuted a new relationship via a carefully cropped—but impressively muscular—bicep. And who could forget her reign during the era of life hacks? Following her rebrand from well-travelled party girl to woke Byron Bay slacktivist, she undoubtedly helped tens of people to understand the benefits of *just five minutes of meditation a day.*

And let's not forget her professional presence. Skilfully, she skirted becoming fully cringeworthy on LinkedIn by subtly including references to her success in carefully written, 'value-adding' thought-leadership posts and infographics that were somewhat actually useful—a talent rarely witnessed on the platform.

And despite her previous existential meltdowns—deleting social media only to redownload it weeks later—she has so far survived scorching her retinas into oblivion with her ring light, 11 409 post re-writes and an inbox full of 'exclusive' offers, only to now succumb to yet another dead phone battery.

In lieu of flowers, followers are asked to like, comment, share and whisper 'link in bio' at sunset. A digital memorial will be held at 7 pm, where guests are encouraged to reshare their favourite reel to their story with the tag #RememberingAlexis.

Alexis may be gone (offline), but her (minimal) legacy lives on in every aesthetically pleasing sunrise, every passive-aggressive satirical caption and every Canva-templated infographic that dares to rework someone else's expertise for social clout.

She came, she posted, she … had an existential meltdown.

It is with heavy thumbs and an out-of-storage iCloud account that we say goodbye to Alexis Zahner on social media: 3500 Instagram followers, 25 000 LinkedIn followers, 1200 Facebook friends, 11 259 status updates. Gone, and quickly forgotten.

Preface

Hi—I'm Alexis, and I'm an addict. A social media addict to be exact. On the surface it doesn't look like a problem, but for the past 20 years I haven't made a single decision that was entirely my own. I've been under the influence—incapable of going a day without some form of interaction with social media. I've come to realise—through an existential crisis, no less—how I've been using social media as a net-negative, and I'd like my life back, free from the invisible shackles of social media influence.

As a millennial, I grew up on the precipice of technology and social media. A tech-free childhood meant establishing the fundamental elements of my self-identity without it. Through adolescence, however, social media entered the chat—and it's been there ever since. It's through this unique perspective that I've experienced the pervasive manner by which social media has become ingrained in who we are and how we live. Social media—an ironic term in and of itself—has contributed more to the epidemic of loneliness in the Western world than any other change in history. It's gone from being a vehicle for connecting people to supplementing real connection altogether. It's now so deeply intertwined in our lives that we can't separate 'real life' from online.

I've personally experienced what would diagnosably be referred to as social media addiction: an inability to put social media apps down for more than minutes at a time. As a result, my concentration and ability to perform basic tasks in my job, home and relationships has suffered. I've found myself struggling to be present in the company of others, despite craving connection and belonging, and found myself experiencing ever-present anxiety, with no clear trigger or cause. My decision making warped as my sense of self became synonymous with my social media presence—an always on, always performing projection of me.

Despite growing up with better life conditions than most generations before us, we're more stressed, lonely and depressed than ever before. So, what are we getting wrong?

To fully understand the impact of social media, I decided to conduct my own experiment: spend a year without any social media, fully disconnecting from Instagram, Facebook, instant messaging services and TikTok. I'd never used online dating platforms but it's important to note I wasn't on those either. The goal was simple: to live in the *real* world, untangling myself from my social media and reconnecting to myself. I knew this kind of clarity wouldn't come from an algorithmically optimised platform fuelled by likes and lies.

I wanted to be able to answer the questions:

- Who am I?
- What do I actually enjoy doing when no-one is watching?
- How do I truly feel connected to the people around me and in my community?

I failed. After a mere six months, I was back on social media. But what I'd uncovered was a gift. I had a new-found perspective on my relationship with social media. My break from it allowed me to recalibrate what a values-aligned life looks like, and where social media fits into that picture. It's allowed me the space to rethink how I live a life of purpose, joy and fulfilment with less comparison, external influence and loneliness.

This book is a coalescence of my story back to myself—in real life—alongside scientific research and evidence-based insights that will support you to reconnect to yourself in a world of social media influence. My goal is simple: to translate what science knows about social media, identity, relationships and wellbeing, and create a resource that is easily accessible for everyone. In this book, you'll encounter sections of anecdote, references to research and studies, diagrams and charts to help you make sense of this information, and practical exercises to support your journey.

This is *Real*, the trials and tribulations of my messy journey to reconnect with myself in a world of likes and lies.

Introduction

I stood staring out at the deep turquoise-blue water of a private Maldivian atoll, a place I'd only ever seen in photos. The water was so clear that I could see coloured coral beneath the surface, alongside even brighter fish. It's a scene you can't believe until you glimpse it with your own two eyes—one that instantly becomes a core life memory, where time stands still as awe and disbelief eclipse rational thought.

Except… the first thought that crossed my mind was how incredible my Instagram carousel was going to look, and how exactly I would caption it to create the best chance of it going viral. Where I should have felt a calm sense of presence and gratitude, instead my stomach swelled with butterflies, a building sense of restlessness and excitement that came from imagining the potential stream of endless likes and comments I would soon relish. As my excitement rose to a fever pitch, I pulled my newly purchased iPhone from my pocket—bought specifically for this purpose—and began busily framing the best shots, my attention slipping rapidly from the scene in front of my eyes to viewing it through the tiny four-inch screen.

'From where you'd rather be? #thisisliving shell-emoji,' I thought dreamily, but that's getting cringey and overused. Perhaps something a little more aspirational, I mused, like, 'Working hard to make my dreams come true' #livingthedream jet-emoji money-emoji. Yet, in actuality, I had just quit my journalism job to travel the world on a shoestring in the midst of my quarter-life existential crisis. 'Damn it,' I wondered, 'why is it so hard to caption this moment perfectly?' I wanted it to feel authentic and offhanded but still show I was doing something extraordinary. Make it understated and cool like this is just who I am, I'm not trying that hard…

'Alexis…'

My inner monologue continued. 'Wait, what if I got lower to the water to take this photo?'

Another call of 'ALEXIS…' came, louder this time.

The jolt of sound pulled me back into time and space like a slap to the face; with a snap of awareness, I re-entered the 'real world'. My then-boyfriend stared at me in a mix of disbelief and mild disdain.

'You are *literally* missing the most beautiful sunset on earth,' he said with an edge of condescension that immediately made me feel equal parts stupid and infuriated.

I turned my attention back towards the horizon to find the sunset had slipped away beneath the impossibly turquoise water and slowly faded to darkness. In my flurry of trying to capture the moment on social media, I'd forgotten to *actually be* there. I'd forgotten to stop and take in the very thing I'd come here to see—that *priceless* view. In my busyness, obsessing over what I was going to post to Instagram, I'd forgotten to live in the actual moment right in front of me. I'd wasted my first Maldivian sunset staring at it through an iPhone screen. How many Maldivian sunsets would I get to experience in this lifetime? The thought suddenly felt depressing. Well, one less now that I'd wasted that first one.

I'd like to report that this moment was a juncture in time where I'd had a revelatory awakening—the realisation that my life was slipping away while I was busy obsessing over my social-media self. Except it wasn't. I then sat distractedly in regret and frustration through my first exquisite seafood dinner on that Maldivian island, internally berating myself for being too caught up on my phone to enjoy my surroundings. I was unconsciously recreating the same pattern I'd repeated a thousand, if not a million, times before. It was just another moment in time when I'd forgotten to live in the real world and got sucked into the vortex of living my life vicariously through my social media self.

This very scenario played out again and again. Always the same lesson, always remaining unlearnt. In fact, this book may have been published years earlier had I managed to find and maintain the courage to rid my life of social media altogether so I could actually focus. But we're here now, and that's what matters.

My 'toxic relationship' with social media plagued my life for a decade. It was an on-again, off-again, complex dynamic where I didn't really want it in my life, but I had no idea how to live without it. I was addicted to the attention and the gratification it gave me. It was like the ability to love-bomb myself: with a perfectly witty caption and a carousel of heavily edited 'candid' images (that took about 200 shots to get right), I could set my (extremely small) following alight. The stream of likes and comments flooded me with a temporary sense of relevance; people were seeing me and I mattered. Social media was the dopamine hit I needed when things in life felt hard. Social media gave me the ability to be whoever I wanted to be—a version of me that was prettier, well travelled, successful and always having a good time. Contrast this with the stark reality of adulthood we all face, where we wonder: Am I good enough? Successful enough? Worthy enough? Pretty enough? Rich enough? Fit enough? The list goes on. And despite what many of us choose to portray on social media, we never *really* feel enough of any of these.

What I started to notice as I unravelled existentially through my twenties was that social media had covertly guided me in a multitude of ways, and I hadn't even noticed. As these moments—like the one in the Maldives—started to register more and more in my conscious awareness, I became acutely aware of how much of life I had *forgotten* to live. I'd become too distracted. I no longer knew who I truly was, what I actually enjoyed doing or who I wanted to spend my time with when the internet wasn't watching. I started to ask myself deeper, more uncomfortable questions: 'Was I even living a life that was of my making? Or was it just a façade for attention and relevance?'

Every time I pondered these questions, I felt a deep sense of hopelessness and confusion sweep over me. Maybe I'm not even in control of these decisions, I'd wonder, but who was calling the shots if not me? At that moment of internal introspection, a realisation occurred: my relationship with social media had gone well beyond healthy. It was subversively and coercively controlling my every decision. From the shoes I wore to the 'type' of boyfriend I wanted to have, I had reduced my life to a series of tick-boxes that I felt would make for an 'Insta-worthy' existence.

The tipping point came some years after the Maldives incident when, under the influence of a social media 'expert', I was doing a goal-setting exercise for the new year. We were tabling our achievements from the previous year and how they made us feel. As I wrote down everything I'd done, I began to notice a sense of hollowness … I had achieved everything I'd said I wanted to and yet I still felt a void inside me. Then it dawned: maybe it was because these goals weren't even my own? They were a product of external influence. And even when I achieved what I thought I wanted, everyone else felt constantly ahead of me anyway. These weren't my goals; they were the goals of 'the internet'—to make $X, to travel to X number of places, to fit X size of clothing—arbitrary, meaningless goals that were rooted in appearances; things I could show on social media with proof; things other people could like and comment on. They didn't come from me at all, and I felt no real sense of pride because they were completely inconsequential.

At that moment, something splintered inside me: it didn't matter what I did or how hard I tried—if I continued comparing myself to everyone on social media I would remain on this treadmill of striving forever and never arrive. I'd never be good enough. It was the moment I realised how thoroughly and profoundly social media had hooked me. Through the constant bombardment of influence, the continuous thirst for validation, I had forgotten what was *truly* important. I'd forgotten to be me. I'd forgotten to really live. To be *real.* And although I didn't know how I was going to fix this, I knew I wouldn't find the answer on social media.

For those of us who've grown up as digital natives, this experience is not an uncommon one. And yet, despite the plethora of information available at our fingertips, we still struggle with what to do about it. Social media—for better or worse—is a part of modern life. It is so deeply ingrained in how we live, who we are and what we do that oftentimes it's hard to draw a line in the sand between our online and offline lives.

After my revelation—that even achieving goals I had set for myself still left me miserable and unfulfilled—I finally recognised the only variable I was yet to tweak in my life was my relationship with social media. And it was at this juncture everything changed. As I set out to unpack what had become an unhealthy relationship with social media—to peel back the layers of influence—I realised I was uniquely positioned to create something from my experience that could benefit others, too.

I've written *Real* because I've lived on both sides of the screen. I occupy a rare proximity to the problem: I'm a millennial who grew up immersed in social media, professionally embedded in the industries that use these platforms to influence and sell, and academically trained to understand their psychological impact. With a master's degree in business psychology and over a decade in marketing and communications, I've built brands from the inside—leveraging the same platforms designed to capture our attention and shape our behaviour. I understand how the architecture works: the emotional hooks, the algorithmic reinforcement, the habit-forming designs that keeps us scrolling long after our intention fades. I've used these tools to grow audiences and sell services, all while trying to shield myself from their effects—my failure to fully do so feels like a karmic irony.

I know this tension isn't unique to me. We all sense the mental health and wellbeing trade-offs of using social media, yet we remain under the influence. *Real* was born from that contradiction—a desire to create a blueprint for reconnecting to myself and reclaiming my agency from this ubiquitous problem plaguing modern life.

My hope is that *Real* serves to reconnect you to the most important person in your life: you.

PART I
The Digital Self

Social media plays a fundamental role in how we see ourselves and our place in the world around us. This part explores identity development, and how, in the modern 'profile era', our performance online has come to be our most outward expression of self.

But is this identity expression of our own volition, or are we just a product of influence? What does *real* look like in an environment of algorithms, content curation and self-objectification?

Together, we'll explore how identity is developed, hijacked and fragmented by social media platforms.

1

Who Am I?

When I was 21, my father passed away quite suddenly, shockingly. On behalf of my family, I made a speech at his funeral. It was the hardest thing I've ever done, and the first time in my life my own mortality felt entirely fragile. I remember grappling with the idea of summarising a person's entire existence — a ridiculous and impossible task. How can 56 years of my father's life — all that he was, that he contributed, that he meant — be reduced to just a few words on a page? How could I do him and his legacy justice? My father was a kind and loving dad and, because of that, I had a childhood full of beautiful memories. Somehow, despite my words never feeling like they were enough, I was able to articulate his incredible impact and the legacy that he left behind.

Since then, I've become obsessed with the idea of my own legacy. What would people say about me if I were no longer here? And what if that time ran out sooner than expected — have I done enough? It's a thought that's plagued me: something I've ruminated on so much it's become an internal compass for my decision making, for better or worse. It's this fear — the fear of not having contributed enough in this life — that led me to totally rethink my relationship with social media.

I could foresee the trajectory of what my relationship with social media would become if left uninterrogated—something shallow, hollow and entirely vanity-driven. It would leave me a shadow of the person I could have become. And the idea of that legacy terrified me. This epiphany showed me that I needed perspective to better calibrate who I was becoming.

Legacy. It's a word we often don't think about until we're much older, or perhaps when it's too late. But if losing my father young taught me anything, it's that we only have one chance to truly live this life of ours—and I'll be damned if I'm going to waste it doomscrolling reels.

Our legacy is the summation of who we choose to be, every day. It's not something that happens by chance, and we certainly shouldn't wait to consider this when we're older. Legacy is intentionally crafted by the decisions we make today. It's the imprint we leave on the world. So we'll begin at the end: are you becoming someone you'd be proud of at 80 years old, if you're privileged to live that long?

The science of 'Who am I?'

At the beginning of 2024, I decided to remove myself from social media entirely… and I began unravelling. Without social media—the constant DMs, meme-sharing and group chats—I felt adrift, separated from everyone else. I lost my sense of self, and I didn't know where or how to find it again. I started asking myself, 'What is truly important to me? What do I value? What relationships bring me joy?' I figured if I could answer these questions, I'd be able to fill the void that had been hollowed out inside me—the persistent shallow feeling that had developed after years of meaningless social media validation. But, as I began to detangle myself from social media, I discovered that my concept of self ran much deeper than this. An existential question emerged: 'Who am I?' (And my next thought was, 'What the hell has social media done to me?')

'Who am I?' is a question we ask in quiet moments and in crisis—and I was firmly experiencing the latter. But it's a question that has been reshaped through time by culture, community and, now, algorithms. Today, the question doesn't live in a journal; it lives in tiny squares on an Instagram feed, bios, search results, status updates and vlogs. To answer this question, we must understand the psychological architecture of the self—and how, in the digital age, that architecture is being constantly renovated in real time.

But to truly try and answer the question of who we are, we need to peel back the layers that make up the 'self'. To do this, I turned to science, philosophy and sociology for an explanation. I needed to feel there was something deeper to who I was than just the aesthetically curated grid of my Instagram profile.

• • •

The self is a system of beliefs, feelings and perceptions that shape how we see ourselves and act in the world. It's not just who we are but who we *think* we are, and how that perception becomes a self-fulfilling loop. The early sociologist Charles Horton Cooley described the self as, 'I am not what I think I am and I am not what you think I am. I am what I think you think I am.'

In short: your identity is a complex, multi-layered and fluid concept that relies both on your perception of self and how you perceive others see you. Complicated, I know.

So, to understand the impact social media has on identity, we first need to dive inwards to understand how our identity is formed.

At the very core of identity is your *self-concept*: your fundamental perception of what makes you who you are. It's who you believe yourself to be. This is composed of the personality traits, characteristics, skills and attributes that make you uniquely you. It's the innermost layer of you—your foundational beliefs about who you are. But self-concept isn't static; it's fluid. It develops and shapes over time, from infancy through to adulthood.

Our self-concept is where we develop our individuality, and it's the basis we use to judge, compare and contrast ourselves in the world among everyone else. Although it becomes more stable throughout our lives, our self-concept remains malleable—continuing to shift and evolve, particularly if we intentionally want it to (more on that later).

The next layer is *self-schema*: the mental filters you use to interpret yourself and the world around you. Imagine a self-schema like you're wearing different pairs of glasses in different scenarios, with each pair filtering information in a slightly different light, influencing how you see yourself in that domain. It's your brain's way of processing and organising information about yourself in different domains, like intelligence, appearance and social ability. For example, if you believe yourself to be generally sociable, you might think, 'I'm someone who makes friends easily.' However, when you apply a negative filter to a context, this can become a self-fulfilling prophecy in action—what you choose to believe about yourself becomes your reality. For example, if you believe you're not very savvy with money, this creates a mental barrier to changing your behaviour, further reinforcing the belief. These mental filters can be hard to spot and change, but we can challenge and interrogate them to reframe them more productively.

Self-concept and self-schema are your innermost layers of self—defining who you believe yourself to be and the filters that protect that concept. The next layers of self are your *self-esteem* and *self-efficacy*. Your self-esteem is how you *feel* about yourself, and your self-efficacy is how you *function* as a result. These become core predictors of how you see yourself—your confidence, fear of failure, resistance to change, tolerance to risk—and will either give rise to personal resilience in the face of setbacks, or not. In short: low levels of self-esteem and self-efficacy mean you don't feel worthy or capable. High levels of self-esteem and self-efficacy mean you feel worthy and capable—you believe in yourself. You can think of this as a simple equation:

Self-belief = Self-esteem (worth) + Self-efficacy (capability)

Your *self-belief* directly impacts *how you behave*, the *habits* you form and your resulting *identity*.

Your behaviours and habits are an outward reinforcement of what you believe to be true about yourself. When you act in the same way repeatedly, this becomes your identity. 'We are what we repeatedly do,' historian Will Durant famously summarised of Aristotle's philosophy, and so 'excellence, then, is not an act, but a habit.' In that vein, your actions can also reinforce a negative self-concept, keeping you stuck in patterns that prohibit growth and expansion.

Here's an example of when a core belief in your self-concept, when appraised negatively, creates a self-fulfilling prophecy that keeps you stuck in a loop:

1. If you believe yourself to be introverted (*self-concept*), you might
2. think yourself bad at making small talk in social settings (*self-schema*). This might result in
3. a lack of confidence when faced with new social circles (*self-efficacy*), and
4. feeling stupid when you're not able to socialise as easily as other people (*self-esteem*), causing you to

5. act awkwardly when meeting people for the first time (*behaviour*), which reinforces
6. the view that 'I'm shy and a naturally unsociable person' (*identity*).

And the loop informs your behaviour, which is fated to repeat.

If your self-schema views your introversion through a different lens, however, this scenario might play out totally differently. For example:

1. If you believe yourself to be introverted (*self-concept*), you might
2. see yourself as someone who forms deep, thoughtful connections rather than thriving on small talk (*self-schema*). This might give you
3. the confidence to focus on meaningful one-on-one interactions when meeting new people (*self-efficacy*), and
4. a sense of pride in your ability to listen and be present (*self-esteem*). As a result,
5. you show up in social situations with calm and genuineness (*behaviour*), which reinforces
6. the view that 'I'm a grounded, thoughtful person who connects deeply, even if I'm not the loudest in the room' (*identity*).

This is how identity becomes a loop: what you *believe* about yourself determines your actions, and your actions reinforce your identity. *You become who you believe yourself to be.*

There are two critical caveats here:

- The first is that self-concept and identity have a *bi-directional* relationship. This means that, over time, intentionally focusing on shifting identity by changing behaviours can reprogram your self-concept (we'll cover this in more depth in Chapter 5).
- The second is that identity isn't a purely introspective concept developed in a vacuum. We rely on feedback from the external

environment to calibrate identity, so how others perceive you impacts how you see yourself in relation to the world. This is where self-concept becomes more complex.

Figure 1.1 shows a simple way of understanding the relationship between how you perceive yourself, how this influences your habits and behaviour, and how this gradually reshapes who you become. It also illustrates the bi-directional relationship between self-concept and identity—how the messages we internalise about our identity can impact our behaviour and our self-concept.

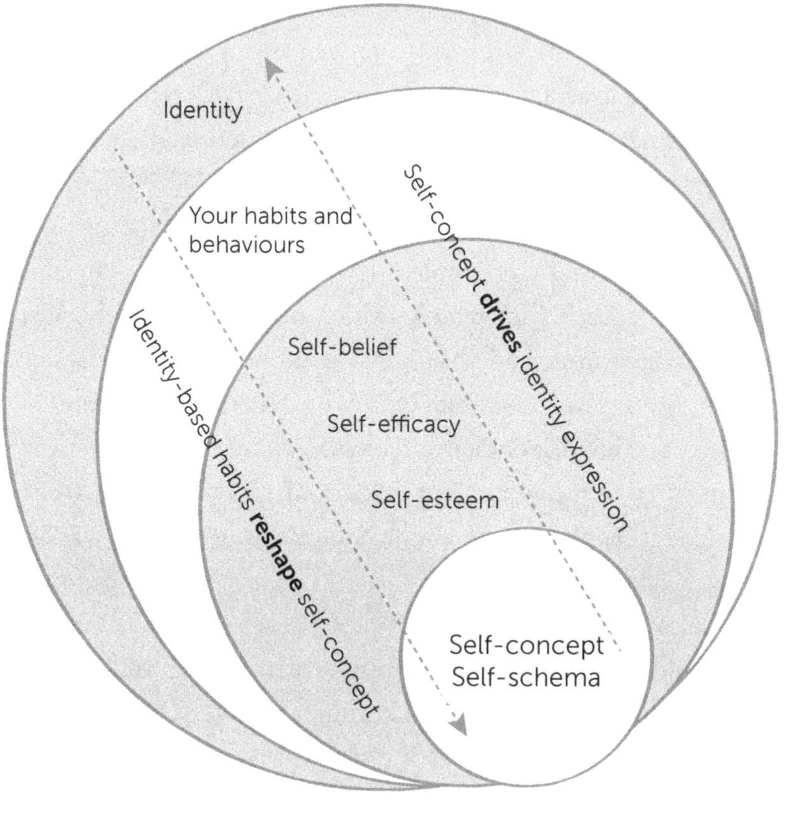

Figure 1.1 The layers of 'self', from self-concept at the innermost core to your identity, which is the outer layer that you project publicly.

We all carry multiple versions of ourselves: who we *actually* are, who we *wish* we were and who we feel we *should* be. Most of us spend a lifetime striving to become an aspirational version of ourselves, while conforming to some degree to the version expected of us, causing us to live in continuous tension. This is natural—striving to evolve ourselves is how we grow. Social media is the home of these aspirational selves. It's where we project and promote the idealised version of ourselves, and see that idealised version of others—when, in reality, none of us embody that version of ourselves all the time. This constant comparison between the 'perfect' people we see online and our everyday selves only amplifies the tension that exists between who we feel we actually are, and who we think we should be. It goes beyond reasonable aspirations and creates an unbridgeable chasm—an unrealistic expectation that we nonetheless internalise and which leaves us feeling we're never quite good enough.

When I began to understand and apply this science to my own behaviours, I realised two things: that I was reinforcing an identity that felt incongruent with who I wanted to become and the legacy I want to leave behind, and that I was quickly becoming the version of myself the internet wanted me to be. Through my fixation on projecting my idealised identity on social media, I was allowing my identity to be judged, scrutinised and dictated solely from the outside-in, rather than from the inside-out. My identity was online mimicry ... not the *real* me.

The following table shows examples at each 'layer' of self—both enabling and limiting manifestations—of thinking and behaviour. From your innermost self-concept through to how you project this as your identity, how you see yourself influences whether you feel enabled or limited by your abilities.

Level	Definition	Function	Enabling example	Limiting example
Self-concept	Your internal belief system	You act in ways that align with who you believe you are	*I am a capable person*	*I'm not good at handling pressure*
Self-schema	Your mental filters	You interpret the world around you according to how you view yourself	*I'm someone who makes friends easily*	*I'm not very savvy with technology or digital things*
Self-esteem	Your worth	You believe you hold innate value (high or low)	*I deserve to be loved and respected*	*I'm not really worth people's time*
Self-efficacy	Your confidence in your abilities	You believe in your ability to take action and achieve outcomes	*I can handle whatever challenges come up at work*	*I always mess things up when the pressure's on*
Self-belief	Your self-trust	Your overarching trust in yourself	*I trust myself to make good decisions, even under stress*	*I always second-guess myself and need outside reassurance*
Behaviour	Your actions	What you do and say as a result, day to day	*I take initiative and follow through on commitments*	*I avoid situations where I might fail*
Habits	Your repeated actions	The patterns you repeat consistently	*I start the day with intention and stay off my phone until 10 am*	*I scroll TikTok every night even when I'm exhausted*
Identity	Who you become as a result	The integrated story and role you live into	*I'm a calm, grounded person who lives by my values*	*I'm scattered, reactive and never fully present*

'Who am I?' isn't a new question

Who am I? is a question human beings have asked for millennia. It's a question I've asked myself countless times—though never more urgently than in the early days after removing myself from social media. The void that followed created space to reflect not only on my social media habits but also on who I was without them.

To understand how social media shapes our identity today, it's helpful to explore how the idea of 'self' has evolved through history—and how, in the 21st century, it has undergone a radical transformation that modern-day philosophers call *the age of the profile self*.

Some of the earliest conceptions of self came from Eastern spiritual traditions. In Hinduism, the *atman*—the true self—is considered to be an eternal, unchanging essence. In contrast, Buddhism proposed that the self is an illusion: a transient, ever-shifting combination of perceptions and sensations. In both, the self isn't something to express or promote; instead, it is something to transcend.

Greek philosophy brought self-awareness into focus. According to Plato, Socrates emphasised introspection, stating that 'the unexamined life is not worth living'. Plato and Aristotle built on this, viewing the self as a composite of reason, emotion and moral action—fulfilling its purpose (or *telos*) through virtue.

During the medieval period, identity was tied to one's place in a divine order. To ask 'Who am I?' was to ask about one's relationship to God, morality and sin. In the Renaissance, selfhood turned inwards and became expressive. Individuals were artists of their lives, crafting their identity through creativity and personal exploration.

Then came the Enlightenment, with Immanuel Kant declaring that we are autonomous beings capable of shaping ourselves through reason and ethics. The modern self became agentic: something we do, not just something we are. Kant believed that human dignity stemmed from our ability to act morally out of duty, guided by principles we gave ourselves. His famous dictum, '*Sapere aude*' (dare to know), captured the Enlightenment ideal: to be human is to rise above instinct and act with reasoned integrity.

But by the 19th century, this idea of a rational, morally grounded self met its fiercest critic: Friedrich Nietzsche. Where Kant saw freedom in rational self-rule, Nietzsche saw repression—a denial of instinct, emotion and creativity. He argued that the modern self had become constrained by morality, guilt and conformity. Instead of discovering a 'true self' through reason, Nietzsche proposed we must *create* ourselves through instinctual acts of becoming. He called for the rise of the *Übermensch*—a figure who rejects herd values and carves out meaning through overcoming their limitations and their expression of personal values.

Together, Kant and Nietzsche represent a deep tension that still echoes today: Is identity something we *cultivate through discipline*, or something we *express through liberation*? Are we meant to follow inner principles, or break them in pursuit of reinvention? Or is it a balance of both?

In the 20th century, modern psychology offered new models. Freud introduced the ego as a way to understand the psyche, how we reason and what drives behaviour. Later, social psychologists reframed the self as being socially constructed. Charles Horton Cooley's concept of the 'looking-glass self' explained that we see ourselves through the imagined eyes of others. Sociologist Erving Goffman then famously proposed that identity is performative: like actors on a stage, we present different versions of ourselves based on the audience before us.

Goffman distinguished between the 'front stage' and 'back stage' identities we all portray:

- **Front stage:** where we perform polished, socially acceptable selves
- **Back stage:** where we relax into our more private, unfiltered selves

This idea helped us understand the fluidity of identity across social contexts. But even Goffman couldn't have anticipated what was coming next.

The digital self

In today's world, our performances are no longer limited to specific moments or social groups. The digital era, and particularly social media, has dissolved the boundary between front stage and back stage. We now curate our identities, constantly, for an audience that is endless, imagined and algorithmically optimised.

This is where philosophers Hans-Georg Moeller and Paul D'Ambrosio offer perhaps the most critical update to understanding selfhood. In their book *You and Your Profile*, they argue that we have moved beyond both the sincere self (aligned with our social roles) and the authentic self (aligned with an inner truth) into the age of the profile self—a concept they call *profilicity*.

In previous eras, we were defined by the roles we fulfilled: son, farmer, mother, priest. The focus for identity was on faithfully embodying what the role demanded. You behaved in alignment with what was expected of that role. In the modern age—from the early 20th century—we shifted to authenticity: the idea that we should be true to some inner essence and resist the social pressure of role conformity in favour of 'being ourselves'.

Today, in the *profile era*, identity is at its most complex yet. Identity is now constructed through what sociologist Niklas Luhmann calls *second-order observation*: we observe how others observe us, then make decisions on our identity accordingly. In other words, we curate ourselves to meet the perceived social expectations others have of us. This is evident in how carefully we consider and frantically update our

Instagram and professional platform bios, and the type of content we choose to share—down to the pictures we use on dating profiles. The question is no longer 'Who am I?' but 'How do I appear?' We've gone from seeking to be *authentic* to needing to be *interesting*.

Moeller and D'Ambrosio's idea of the *profile self* is far from a private, introspective being, but instead a public-facing, reputational construct. It's your very own personal *brand*, designed for algorithmic recognition, professional advancement and social validation. We're optimising ourselves for public consumption. Where we used to play roles based on context; the profile self is instead structured, persistent and portable across time and platforms. We are no longer just acting in scenes for the people directly in front of us; we are building entire personal brands, based on how we perceive others to be perceiving us, and then attempting to manipulate this perception. And yes, I realise that does sound like the plot of the 2010 film *Inception*...

This transformation of identity has profound consequences. It shifts our attention from introspection to presentation; from an internal compass of moral coherence to aesthetic curation; and from self-knowledge to audience engagement and optimisation. We're becoming dancing monkeys for the faceless algorithms. As the profile self becomes the primary vehicle of our selfhood, the danger lies in believing we *are* our profile.

Here's the irony: the more we try to appear authentic online, the more we become performative. As Moeller and D'Ambrosio note in their earlier book *Genuine Pretending*, all identity is an act of performance. The illusion isn't in the performance but in believing that there is an 'authentic self' somewhere behind it. Citing Chinese philosopher Zhuangzi (also known as Zhuang Zhou), they suggest that rather than clinging to a fixed identity and deeming that to be authentic—such as the version of ourself we present in a digital profile—we should aim to become better pretenders: people who perform that self in varying contexts with gentle detachment, awareness, fluidity and morals.

I'll admit that when I first tried to make sense of this philosophy, I was baffled. But soon I came to realise that perhaps the question of 'Who am I?' in the digital age isn't about uncovering some buried inner truth but about noticing the pattern of our performance. It evolves the question to 'Who am I pretending to be, and why? And does this pattern of performance lead me closer to the person I want to become?'

In a digital world, where performance feels omnipresent, this shift to a carefully curated profile self carries a heavy psychological weight. We're now always on, always pretending, always dancing for the algorithm. This challenges how we think about our attention and agency, and the possibility of being at home in ourselves when a version of us is always on display.

Before we can break this cycle, we first need to understand how it functions and its cost.

2

Selfies, Filters and Self-Objectification

I sprang out of bed with just enough time to make it to the tiny all-in-one shower and toilet in our villa before vomiting violently and slumping against the toilet bowl. For the third day in a row, I was bedridden, passing in and out of a sweat-soaked consciousness with a fever, a splitting headache and a relentless stomach upset—I'll spare you the full details. As I lay on the cold tiles, I thought to myself: 'I'd pay anything to get off this *expletive* island.' Eventually, after more profanity, ugly crying and an unanswered prayer, I crawled back to bed. Habitually, I picked up my phone and scrolled Instagram—a much-needed distraction from my current reality—and thankfully, there on the tiny screen, the dopamine hit I desperately needed was delivered. As I opened the Instagram app I was met with a slew of fresh comments and likes on my most recent post: a sunset cocktail at a nearby beach resort, backlit by the Maldivian sunset, declaring #thisisliving.

It was a photo taken days earlier, a momentary escape from my dreary reality before I was struck down by whatever gut bug had likely crept into the crushed ice of said cocktail. But I couldn't show that side of my 'luxurious trip' to my followers.

In truth, we weren't staying in that fancy resort; we were staying at a budget villa down the road. A villa I hadn't left the confines of for three days—hardly Insta-worthy. But the post was *technically* true: I had been there, in that place, drinking a cocktail at sunset. I was just strategically presenting a side of events that was more glamorous than reality. Was that so wrong? It wasn't a lie, just a version of the truth. It was a moment when I realised how performative I'd become: my followers weren't really seeing me, they were seeing my carefree, glamorous, well-travelled self—my *profile self*. And that profile self was a highlight reel only.

While the instinct to perform is a normal part of being human, in this profile era it's supercharged. On social media, the curtain never closes; the stage is always waiting, the audience ever-present, and the performance is constant. Even our backstage moments become part of the performance—an opportunity to spruik 'authenticity' as the pressure to curate the *right* impression feels ever-demanding.

We've moved beyond just performing roles in specific contexts into constructing enduring, always-on, algorithmically optimised profiles. And these profiles go well beyond our social roles. They're public-facing brands; they're identity commodified. We're not just performing, we're *brand building*. And we're no longer judged by our integrity or sincerity, but by how interesting, relevant or aesthetically pleasing we appear to others.

In essence, this is performative behaviour: the curation of an idealised self for public consumption, and psychologists call this *impression management*—crafting how others see us. In the digital era, impression management has become our default because visibility and influence is the new currency. We consciously do it, by curating our profiles through what we share, but we unconsciously do it, too, when we habitually filter out the messy, non-Insta-worthy parts of our lives. And this comes at an often unseen cost.

When we're constantly performing for a faceless audience—especially one shaped by algorithms—the lines between the profile self and who we are outside of this blur. Our identity becomes entangled with the profile self.

Constant performance erodes spontaneity and joy within the moment too, because we're often contemplating how to *present* the moment, and how that will be perceived by an online following—robbing us of the opportunity to be present in it.

And because our online audience amalgamates our social groups into one undifferentiated mass—from coworkers to family, friends to strangers, prospective employers to prospective partners—we're forced to assume a palatable middle-ground persona, suitable for the consumption of all. Researchers call this phenomena *context collapse*: the merging of all audiences into a singular group. This amplifies the performance pressure, forcing us to become more generic, controlled, *vanilla*—expressing only what seems safe or impressive, rather than true.

In this way, the profile self becomes a form of self-preservation. We use performance as a psychological shield against rejection, shame or public scrutiny of our whole self, much like an actor who plays one role on the stage and is altogether different in reality. Except, as our profiled self receives public validation, this curated self doesn't just protect us from scrutiny—it begins to *replace us.*

When we allow the profile self to become the sum total of the whole self, we risk slipping into dark patterns—self-objectification and identity fragmentation—that gradually distort how we see ourselves and reduce us to something less than we are. But why does this matter? Why shouldn't we be the shiny, always-on profile self? Let's unpack it.

The self-objectifying selfie

The selfie has become the defining symbol of the profile era—but what's the darker side to this seemingly innocent photograph? From mirror selfies to filtered stories, the selfie has become a gateway to something more complex and concerning. Where we were once the subject of photographs, we've now become an *object*. The selfie—far from a form of artistic self-expression, with the self as the subject—has become a vessel for validation and social approval. It's a tool for *self-objectification*, where the observer's evaluation is more important than our own.

Psychologists Barbara Fredrickson and Tomi-Ann Roberts defined self-objectification as the tendency to experience our body as an object, something to be viewed and evaluated, rather than as a living, feeling being. It *dehumanises* us. This isn't just about vanity; it's a fundamental shift in our perspective that affects our emotions, cognition and self-worth. Researchers have consistently linked self-objectification to increased anxiety, body shame, disordered eating and reduced mental performance, particularly among women and adolescents.

On visually led platforms like Instagram, Snapchat and TikTok—where we've sanctified physical appearance, aesthetic consistency and curated perfection above all else—self-objectification has become the norm. We've come to accept vanity-first self-presentation without question. As a result, our self-worth has been outsourced for the judgement of others, our value derived from how we appear rather than who we are. We've become reduced to a digital paper doll: flat, filtered, flimsy and fragile. *Fake.* And in doing so, we disconnect from the full spectrum and wonder of our identity—our humour, creativity, intelligence, empathy and character. The *real.*

But self-objectification didn't begin with social media. For centuries, we've compared ourselves to others, sought social acceptance and modified our appearance to attract attention and affection. From an evolutionary perspective, this made sense: group acceptance meant the ability to find a mate and survive. But today, these biological drives are co-opted by a pseudo-survival strategy: the pursuit of online validation.

Social media doesn't just reflect these pressures, it amplifies them — turbocharging self-objectification by placing us under constant visual scrutiny, where our worth is measured not by how we feel but by engagement metrics and visibility. The perception of our profile self is tantamount to group acceptance, to our survival — or, at least, it can feel that way.

This regular self-objectification leaves us feeling hollow, disconnected and reliant on external affirmation. We outsource how we feel about ourselves to people we often don't even know. We've become more concerned with how our life *looks*, rather than how it feels to actually *live* it.

And this vulnerability is a target. Just as we're feeling most insecure, social media presents us with a solution — a product, a treatment, an app — just the thing we need to feel better. It's a cycle of algorithmic exploitation: feel inadequate, buy something, experience temporary relief, repeat. Our insecurities are being exploited and monetised by the very platforms that helped create them. And this cycle is fated to repeat itself, as the root cause remains undiagnosed: a distorted self-image shaped by relentless self-objectification, comparison and unrealistic aesthetic pressure.

Filtered beauty and algorithmic ideals

As this performative loop conditions us to objectify ourselves for social applause, it's no surprise that our beauty ideals are being rapidly reshaped by algorithms over reality. The more we post, the smarter the algorithms become, as they learn which faces get likes, which bodies are saved and what looks are reshared. Our self-objectification becomes codified beauty optimisation: we now have a collective, digitised standard of what 'looking good' means. And this standard is anything but realistic.

As a child, my favourite book was a flipbook—the kind where you could switch the hairstyle, shirt, pants and shoes of your favourite character. I'd spend hours switching her style depending on my mood. Party one day, beach trip the next. It was an innocent and tactile form of self-expression: mix-and-match identity play. Except today's flip books are filters. Instead of switching outfits, we're trying on new noses, higher cheekbones, thinner hips, a bustier chest, a darker complexion and smoother skin—there's no end to the appearances we can retrofit using filters. But the crisis begins when the filter fades and the reality of our appearance doesn't match what we're being told it needs to.

As our visual identity has become the primary projection of the self online, we obsess over editing, filtering and upgrading our appearance to conform to what's trending and algorithmically rewarded, which creates yet another layer of outside-in identity distortion.

Philosopher and cultural critic Heather Widdows identified four dominant pillars of contemporary beauty in her research: thinness, firmness, smoothness and youthfulness. And these aren't just trends; they're new standards, reshaping our behaviours, spending and sense of worth. And when they meet the algorithms, they perform, becoming further reinforced through what we like, share and follow, and exposing us to an endless loop of algorithmically idealised beauty. These pillars set standards most of us don't, and can't, meet.

Writer Jia Tolentino calls this the 'Instagram face': a racially ambiguous, hyper-symmetric, plastic-smooth aesthetic that combines features from various ethnicities into one homogenised, filtered ideal. It's a face that no-one naturally has—an impossible coalescence of features that many now pay to achieve through cosmetic enhancement like fillers, enhancements and surgery.

The endless loop of self-objectification, comparison and modification is literally pushing us beyond natural limits and towards algorithmic optimisation. This isn't empowerment; it's conformity to an unrealistic standard. The irony? What's being sold as self-improvement is actually self-erasure.

And all the while we're chasing beauty standards that look aspirational on the outside, our health and wellbeing tend to deteriorate as a result. Achieving these standards often involves restrictive eating, cosmetic surgery, performance-enhancing drugs and expensive 'health' supplements that alter our very physiology.

Sadder still is that this cultural obsession now plagues our youngest generations. Appearance-based bullying is now the most common form of school bullying. We're conditioning children from a young age to compare themselves to impossible standards, like filtered avatars and algorithmically defined beauty standards. Before they've even had a chance to find themselves, we're telling them who they should be. And most fall short of these impossible expectations.

The homogenisation of beauty is making us more anxious, depressed, disconnected and obsessive. Where social media promised tools for self-expression, we've turned them into tools for identity curation. We have no time to be ourselves because we're too busy trying to be everyone else.

We're not trying on identities from a flipbook anymore; instead, the algorithm nudges us towards what's most clickable. But no matter how many times we upgrade our appearance, the picture never quite feels complete.

So, how do we break free? We'll explore that. But first, we need to look at the next trap: how social media fragments our sense of self and encourages us to present it in carefully cropped, socially acceptable pieces.

But before we move on, it's worth asking yourself: when was the last time you did something because it felt good, not because it would look good? In the age of the profile, reclaiming your sense of self begins with that question.

3

Identity Fragmentation, Comparison and Validation

'Woah, that post *literally* blew up my social feed,' I mused to my then-boyfriend over breakfast. After waking up to 100 likes on a heavily edited shot of me lying on a suspended bed over the obscenely turquoise water of the Maldives, I was basking in the short-lived afterglow that instant social validation brings. It was a photograph that took every last ounce of my then-boyfriend's patience, and the entirety of my camera roll space to capture. And in that brief moment, I had felt the rush of gratification—I had been seen and heard, and I'd looked really cool doing it.

But the win was short-lived. Within a few moments, the feeling of elation had passed; I sat there picking at my breakfast absentmindedly, already formulating a plan for another post.

Social media satisfies our human need to be seen, heard, valued and affirmed by giving us the tools to project ourselves into the public domain. Social media platforms reward specific behaviours—polished selfies, glamorous outfits, flaunted muscles, exotic destinations—and we perform these behaviours for the promised rewards. But the reward is more than just validation, it's a dopamine hit too—a neurochemical that makes us feel good—and it hooks us. But the validation we receive is superficial—a cheap form of attention that lacks a deeper sense of fulfilment. Over time, as we chase this validation, it rewires our brains to crave the hollow thrill of likes, comments and reposts, turning our online identity into an addictive loop.

As the writer James Clear outlines in his book *Atomic Habits*, our repeated behaviours become our identity: we form habit loops around what's rewarded on social media. But because our online behaviour is only a fragment of who we are, we hide the parts of us that don't perform well online. We start to allow our profiled self to become the dominant self-story, which is the beginning of *identity fragmentation*.

Identity fragmentation is the splintering of the self into polished, socially acceptable pieces, while hiding or discarding the parts of us that don't fit the ideal. In the profile era, this means curating an idealised version of the self that aligns with our online persona. What Hans-Georg Moeller and Paul D'Ambrosio call the 'profile self' becomes the centre of our identity, overshadowing the complexities of our full humanity. This loop reshapes our internal narrative, pushing us to *be* that version, always. The loop becomes more than just behavioural; it becomes existential.

Imagine you're given a decadent chocolate mud cake, layered with delicious ingredients, most of which are hidden on the inside. You cut a slice—just one—and that slice represents your Insta-worthy, carefully curated profile self: what people see on your profile. Then, you pick up the rest of the cake and throw it in the trash—the rest of the cake represents the parts you don't share on your online profile. But the reality is that the rest of the cake represents the *whole* you: your sense of humour, dreams, fears, values, intelligence, quirks, relationships, culture and so on. If your entire worth is tethered to only one small slice of the cake, then you're forgetting the richness of the whole.

We can apply psychologist E Tory Higgins' *self-discrepancy theory* to help explain this. Self-discrepancy theory explains the emotional discomfort we experience when who we aspire to be and who we are don't align. As the gap widens, our feelings of shame, insecurity and disappointment intensify. Social media continually reminds us of this gap, rewarding our curated self and urging us to keep the unfiltered hidden.

This matters because our identities are *meant* to be messy and complex. Social psychologist Patricia Linville's research in this area found that people with multifaceted identities are more resilient to stress, a concept she calls *self-complexity*. When life inevitably changes—jobs, relationships, friendships, ageing—people with self-complexity have layers of depth to draw on, rather than being anchored to a narrow superficial slice of the whole. Going back to the cake analogy, if you rely on a single slice to define your whole self, then you risk feeling rejected when that slice doesn't perform well online. A whole, layered and complex self supports you and enables you to be more psychologically stable and less fragile, especially in response to the whims of social media.

The problem is the algorithm doesn't reward complexity; instead, it rewards consistency, coercing us to persistently curate our profiled self and discard the rest. And this becomes problematic for a number of reasons.

In addition to reduced self-complexity, there's an emotional cost to keeping up this profile appearance. Dubbed *digital identity fatigue* by researchers, we experience emotional exhaustion as we labour over maintaining a constant curated persona. But because the platforms reward our performance, we double-down anyway—fragmenting ourselves into fragile slices and exhausting ourselves in the process.

In this way, the algorithm becomes a mirror, reflecting back the parts of you that are socially approved while encouraging you to align your real-world identity to this profile self. The more we perform for social media, the more we internalise this performance as being representative of who we are, narrowing our real identity to match the digital brand—a process researchers Nick Yee and Jeremy Bailenson have called the *Proteus effect*.

The result? We become reliant on external feedback to feel good about ourselves and tell us who we are, because who we are has been fragmented into just a small sliver of the whole—the profile self. And as we shift priority from what makes us *feel* good to what *looks* good, we become reliant on the audiences we're trying to impress. When validation slows or, worse, disappears, we interpret this as a personal failure—not just of a social post but of our own self-worth.

It's a dark hole I know all too well.

The comparison trap

By design, social media is about *seeing and being seen* by others. If you think you're able to moderate how this constant social comparison impacts you, you're wrong. Oftentimes its effects are felt as an undercurrent of mood and emotion you can't quite put your finger on. It's like an ambience. And like much of what we've discussed so far, until we bring conscious awareness to it, the repercussions of how social media impacts us go subtly unnoticed.

Social media invokes our natural human mechanism for comparison. Coined by social psychologist Leon Festinger, *social comparison* is how we evaluate ourselves compared to others. It's how we make sense of our own opinions, skills and identity by measuring ourselves against those around us. And it can be motivating and confidence-boosting, in the right dosage. If we compare ourselves to those we perceive to be better than us (upwards comparison), we can feel motivated to strive. Comparing ourselves to those we perceive to be worse off than us (downward comparison) can help us feel more confident in our abilities. But when the balance is off—such as when we're flooded with algorithmically curated highlight reels on social media—we become stuck in constant upward comparison with people who are wealthier, sexier, thinner, fitter and more successful than us, and because it's seemingly *everyone*, this no longer feels motivating; instead, it feels demoralising.

To illustrate how pervasive this is in our modern environment, let's compare your experience to that of your grandparents. Fifty years ago, your grandparents would have likely lived in a community with a diverse set of people: some would have been wealthier than them, with nicer houses and cars, and some would have been worse off. In that community, they would have compared themselves to those 100 families around them to discern their relative social standing. My grandparents were firmly middle class—they lived in a modest house, had modest jobs (my grandfather worked in the railway industry; my grandmother worked as a janitor at a school) and had one family car. They strived to provide a good family life for their children by working hard to afford education and other niceties, like new clothing and shoes, perhaps with the dream that their children would one day live a life better than theirs. Today, you're likely to be more educated, be wealthier and have access to a plethora of experiences your grandparents didn't, and yet you probably feel like that's not good enough. Why? Because you're no longer just comparing your life to those 100 other families in your immediate surroundings. Instead, you're comparing your life to millions of people from across the world, and this is happening *constantly*. The pool from which you can draw comparative data about yourself is quite literally endless and also largely irrelevant to your actual quality of life.

This constant exposure to upward comparison erodes our self-worth and makes us feel less capable. When we're constantly exposed to people who we perceive to be better than us, we start to believe it. Research confirms the more time you spend on social media, the worse you feel about yourself. This is especially true if you're following appearance-focused accounts. One study in particular, by Jasmine Fardouly and colleagues, noted the detrimental effects these types of image-obsessed accounts have on women's perceptions of their appearance and their bodies. The impact weakens our self-concept, and we often don't even realise it's happening.

And don't forget, these comparisons aren't being made between our full selves; instead, we're comparing our curated slice of identity with everyone else's greatest hits, all compiled into highlight reels, which fuels our feelings of inadequacy in a vicious loop—the more inadequate we feel, the deeper our craving for social validation. But instead of stepping back to question the comparison, we get swept up in chasing the validation. We start to mimic the trends and behaviours we see on social media until we're trying to become someone else entirely. What starts as an upward comparison results in us craving validation in an endless loop of never feeling good enough.

Craving validation

As the algorithm super-charges our upward social comparison by showing us more of what we ought to be—brilliant, talented, beautiful and successful people who are seemingly better than us in every way—we internalise these external cues so they mean something *about* us: that we are not good enough as we are, which activates our craving to feel validated on social media's terms.

Validation is the psychological reward social media gives us that we interpret as affirmation of our self-worth. It's social confirmation for behaving and looking a certain way, which is approved by others and the algorithm. Likes, comments and reposts are a form of modern currency and, if we're really worth it, we'll be picked up by the algorithm and promoted further. Think of the thrill of 'going viral'—the ultimate nod of approval in the social media world.

Moeller and D'Ambrosio's profile self explains why this craving is so persistent; in the profile era, our self-worth has shifted from a need for internal alignment to an external, *consistent performance.* Reinforced by invisible algorithmic forces, we create the perfect storm: we compare, curate, get socially rewarded and then double-down on what's being validated.

The more we compare ourselves to idealised people on social media, and continually attempt to keep up, the more we become reliant on this external validation to feel good about ourselves. This becomes dangerous because we're *outsourcing* our self-esteem and self-worth to others. And as we double-down on this performance, rather than really living, we continue to fragment who we are, replacing our internal compass with engagement metrics. Instead of asking ourselves, 'How do I feel?' we ask, 'How do I look to others?', which puts us in a precarious position where we are reliant on the reactions of others to regulate our emotions and confirm our self-worth.

Commitment and consistency bias

As we invest effort into our online persona, we start to feel psychologically committed to that version of ourselves; we feel the weight of being that person and preserving that identity consistently. In his book *Influence: The Psychology of Persuasion*, psychologist Robert Cialdini explains this as our innate desire to behave in a way that aligns with our publicly presented version of self—once we're committed to a public identity, we feel compelled to reinforce it consistently. In social media terms, this translates to being 'on-brand', and the validation we receive for being consistently on-brand reinforces this pressure.

This consistency has repercussions. As we attach ourselves to our online persona, our sense of self becomes more limited and rigid. We become committed to being this *version* of ourselves rather than being open to evolving and growing. Except the more rigidly we perform—aligning to just a slice of our full self—the more fragile we become. This has repercussions for our critical thinking and worldview too, which we'll cover in more detail in Chapter 8 in particular.

When life inevitably changes—you lose a job, change your appearance, grow older, change relationships—you're less resilient to these changes because they create tension within your narrowly curated identity. The more you commit to being your online persona, the less layered and complex your identity becomes.

And while many of us think that curating an online persona is about striving for *authenticity*, we're in fact doing the opposite. The more we strive to consistently curate ourselves, the more fragmented and performative we become (as shown in figure 3.1). This is a paradox of authenticity that we buy into by believing that who we are online is the summation of who we are.

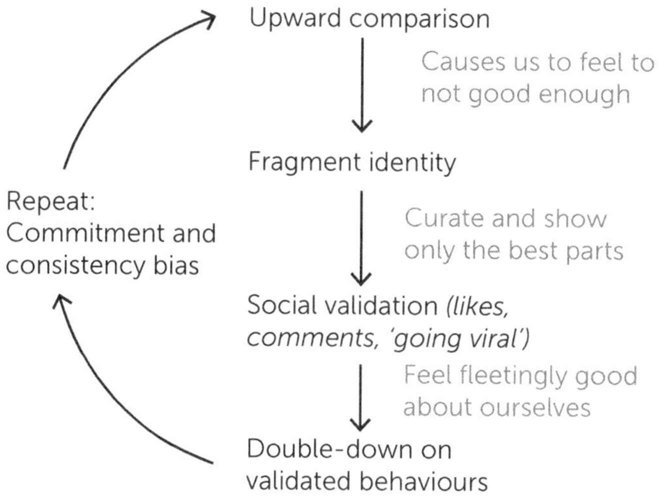

Figure 3.1 The cycle of upward comparison and how it influences us to fragment our identity for social validation. The more we're rewarded with likes, comments and social reward for our social media posts, the more we double-down on these behaviours and repeat them.

4

Authenticity, Performance and the Genuine Fake Paradox

The humidity felt like a weighted blanket; it was stiflingly hot as a friend and I ducked and weaved through the throng of Bangkok street vendors, amid a cacophony of beckoning calls: 'Hey ladies, great prices.' 'Hello girls, special price for you.' After already a month of travelling in Thailand, I barely registered the noise anymore—until I heard, 'Hello ladies, genuine fake Louis Vuitton ... '

I stopped. The oxymoron 'genuine fake' struck a chord. I turned towards the seller, intrigued.

'What do you mean by a *genuine fake*?' I asked him.

A slow grin spread across his face. A *genuine fake*, he explained, meant a real leather bag, expertly made so it looked exactly like the real thing, even though it wasn't. It was counterfeit, but it was in the right price range for two broke backpackers.

Taking the knock-off Louis Vuitton bag from his outstretched hand, I inspected it closely. He was right: the bag could easily pass as the real deal to the unassuming eye. And I was looking at it with the eyes of a 20-something university student on minimum wage who'd never held a *real* designer bag before.

'What else have you got?' I asked, nodding towards his makeshift shop.

Moments later, seated on plastic stools inside the ramshackle store, we were treated to a backstreet fashion parade: from Gucci to Hermès; Prada to Dolce & Gabbana. Bag after bag was being flaunted in front of us. I was amazed. To the unqualified eye, they all looked legitimate, indistinguishable from their high-end counterparts.

Leaving with my very own fake Prada bag, I felt both smug and uneasy, like I'd been let in on a dirty secret. I'd seen young women just like me in nightclubs, at my university campus and on Instagram flaunting designer bags, and I'd always assumed them to be wealthier and more stylish than me. But now I knew: you could cheat yourself into this image. They weren't real—they were genuine fakes. Counterfeits. Inauthentic.

Within the hour, I was uploading my own genuine fake to Instagram—a counterfeit Prada bag and a cocktail in my hand—only to be left feeling a little hollow. I was nothing but an imposter, holding a symbol of status but knowing it was fake. It was a glamorous illusion. And if *anyone* could buy the illusion, then what was the point?

This fateful trip was early in the social media era—2011, to be exact. Facebook's 'Like' button was a mere two years old, Instagram was home to single, static images, SnapChat was about to launch and TikTok was still years from existence. Social media hadn't yet infiltrated every aspect of our lives. There was still a clear delineation between who we were in 'real life' and our social media profiles. Despite this, even in those early days, buying a genuine fake had shifted something in me. I started questioning what I saw—when pictures seemed too perfect, and vulnerability too rehearsed, the idea of a genuine fake became my inner litmus test. I started to believe that inauthenticity was something you could clearly spot.

However, in the decade that followed, the lines completely blurred. We scroll, we share and we perform, and the boundary between our real and online selves has dissolved. Social media no longer reflects real life—it shapes it. And we don't question it, as performing for social media has become second nature. Authenticity is now part of our daily vocabulary, but the term has been popularised by the very platforms that incentivise polish and performance, and encourage us to be genuine fakes ourselves, which raises the question: Is authenticity something that can even exist on social media?

What is authenticity, really?

To understand authenticity, it's helpful to understand its *etymology*: the history and evolution of the word itself. Authenticity traces back to the Greek 'authēntes': derived from 'autos' (self) and 'hentēs' (doer, being), meaning 'one who acts on their own authority'. Humanistic psychologists later defined it as living in alignment with your true self: unedited, values-aligned and free from societal expectation. Through its evolution, it's become synonymous with words like genuine, original and unfiltered. Its antonyms? Fake, imitation, false.

However, when we view authenticity through a psychological and sociological lens, we realise it's far more complicated than this. In his seminal work *Race and Culture*, Robert Ezra Park says that all identity is performance: 'everyone is always and everywhere, more or less consciously, playing a role—we come into the world as individuals, achieve character, and become personas.' According to Park, what begins as a mask, becomes who we are. Now, in our online *profile era*, this has evolved again. We've transitioned to a persistent performance that's curated for algorithms, online audiences and social capital. It's a continuous loop of personal branding, where identity is shaped by the perception of others in online environments. In this current era, authenticity isn't a state of being—it's more like a social media engagement strategy.

So, can we truly be seen as *real* while we're simultaneously curating our lives to fit into neat, Instagrammable squares? Our authenticity—once believed to be a reflection of our innermost truth and integrity—has been co-opted into a performative dance for a global, faceless audience. While we crave to be seen as real, we're instead curating our lives to look and feel a certain way. Authenticity has become something we do, rather than how we are.

As authenticity has become entangled with social pressure, it's given rise to carefully curated personal branding. Where once the goal of authenticity was individual self-expression through our fashion, music and art choices, we're now coerced by algorithmic cues and social comparison to curate a *sense* of authenticity through consistency and conformity.

So, what does it mean to be authentic in the digital age, where self-expression is always mediated through a screen? And should authenticity even be the goal?

The genuine fake paradox

Since that fateful trip to Thailand, the genuine fake concept has lodged itself in my brain like a splinter. You can't unsee what your eyes have been opened to, and I began to recognise it everywhere. Not just in handbags, but in people, social media posts and even myself. I grew increasingly sceptical and uneasy: in a digital world, where performance and perception take priority over personal truth, is anyone truly authentic anymore? And more disturbingly, am I?

The answer: It's complicated.

The tension between authenticity and performance creates a paradox—how can we be authentically ourselves while performing for an audience? By becoming a genuine fake: someone who appears authentic, but whose expression of authenticity is simultaneously performative. We're revealing a *version* of ourselves: one that's curated, filtered and strategically presented for social reward, whether we think we are being authentic or not.

Moeller and D'Ambrosio explored this through the Daoist philosophy of *genuine pretending*, which explains how in some form or another we're always pretending, and this is inherently part of life, so it isn't deceitful but more a natural part of being social creatures. The issue, then, isn't that we perform, but that we believe the illusion that our performance should reveal some pure, true essence underneath. We're trying to convince ourselves of our authenticity while performing—and this creates a feeling of incongruence. Even our moments of vulnerability—the raw and unedited—become part of the show, all carefully curated to posit truthfulness while maintaining a palatable relatability. The paradox isn't that we're fake; it's that we're trapped in needing to *look* real.

The dilemma for us is that social media doesn't reward inner congruence; it rewards the performance of congruence, covertly nudging us to consider how every moment will look, be received and, ultimately, be socially rewarded. In this way, our digital self is contradictory—aspirationally, we want to be authentic, but by virtue of crafting a profile for public consumption we walk a tightrope between being truthful and meeting the pressures of public perception and social acceptance. Authenticity is an illusion, and we've tricked ourselves into believing we can perform it.

Performing authenticity

If authenticity is something we can do, then what makes a person *seem* authentic? When I asked people, the most common theme I heard was 'being *real*'. But it was about more than just appearing real; it was a sense we felt from others. Intrigued, I wanted to uncover the exact ingredients that make us feel authentic to others, in the hope I could find a way to feel more authentic myself.

Psychologists Michael Kernis and Brian Goldman frame authenticity as alignment. In simple terms, this means knowing yourself, understanding what you value and what motivates you, being honest with yourself about your thoughts and feelings, acting in ways that are congruent with these, and being open in your relationships. But in the social media era, this alignment feels out of reach. We often feel inauthentic when using social media because platforms continually nudge us to perform certain parts of ourselves and hide the rest. Our whole authentic self doesn't feel good enough, so authenticity becomes filtered—literally and metaphorically.

Scholars Maureen Ebben and Elizabeth Bull suggest that on social media, authenticity is no longer simply about internal alignment—it's also about performance, context, audience and algorithm. It's co-constructed: we learn to express 'realness' in ways that are socially rewarded, and commercially viable. Authenticity is now something we *do* as much as something we *are*. Which raises the question: Are we being ourselves, or performing the 'self'?

Authenticity in the digital era is as complex as it is premeditated. It is no longer simply 'being yourself'; instead, it's a carefully constructed curation containing glimpses of the self alongside a very deliberate performance—a precise formula revealing just the right dosage of the self for palatable public consumption.

Paradoxically, it's this intentional construction of authenticity that blends the 'real' you with very deliberate self-presentation to create a genuine fake. This becomes a slippery slope when we play the role of both actor and audience, shaping our self-expression off what earns validation. We become enmeshed in the performance, no longer able to distinguish them apart. Over time, the performance begins to feel habitual, maybe even hollow, and the labour of constantly pretending to be real can lead to exhaustion—we experience authenticity fatigue.

Authenticity fatigue arises from the ongoing pressure to appear genuine, transparent and relatable. It occurs when authenticity becomes a performance expectation rather than a personal truth. The effort to maintain a consistent, emotionally expressive and 'real' persona becomes draining and insincere, particularly when it's shaped by audience feedback, algorithms or engagement goals.

Authenticity drives engagement

No-one believes themselves to be 'fake', yet if social media didn't exist, would you still feel the same drive to share the things you post online? Would you knock on a friend's door to show them your new outfit, or recount a story to an audience of strangers? Would you offer unsolicited exercise advice or spiritual guidance to your neighbour? Probably not. This doesn't mean you're insincere; it means social media amplifies our natural performative tendencies. We all curate, but the platform turns even casual sharing into a performance.

To *appear* authentic, we often employ authenticity cues: signals used to create the impression of being real, relatable or emotionally honest. These cues are how we perform authenticity for digital self-presentation. They're strategic behaviours skilfully used to make our online audience feel that we're real. These tactics are very intentionally used among influencers and content creators, but they're now so widely adopted that we all use them every day too—often without realising it.

Common authenticity cues include:

- Sharing personal struggles, vulnerabilities or failures to appear relatable
- Using informal, conversational language to feel approachable

- Disclosing sponsorships or 'being transparent' about partnerships
- Posting raw or 'unedited' content—filtered to look unfiltered
- Expressing strong, consistent personal values or social stances

These cues function as shortcuts to trust. They mimic the conditions of authenticity—alignment, congruence, openness, emotional honesty—but don't necessarily confirm it. In fact, the more these cues are consciously deployed to generate engagement, the more they become a part of the performance of authenticity rather than evidence of it.

And here's where the *genuine fake paradox* intensifies: even when we start with honest intentions, we quickly learn which cues garner more likes, shares and social rewards. So, we begin to shape our content around what works and what drives engagement, reinforcing a subtle drift away from inner alignment and towards audience optimisation. In this way, authenticity becomes not just a state—but a strategy.

The result? The performance becomes so habitual and reflexive that we become it; we forget to ask whether the person we're presenting online still feels like us at all. It's a performance so normal that we lose track of where it began. And when we play the genuine fake for too long, our self-concept becomes shaped by the feedback of our following—from the outside in. The behaviours that are rewarded with engagement increase, and we discard those that aren't—we become ever more the actor.

If you're questioning whether what you post is a genuine fake, ask yourself: 'Would I still do this if no-one saw it? If this post gets no reaction, would I still share it?' If the answer is no, that's not a cause for shame. It's simply a sign of the environment we're in—a space where the perception of authenticity drives engagement.

It's not just us using authenticity as an engagement tactic either. As social media has evolved, authenticity has become a commodity, a currency, something that can be developed and traded. Authenticity now has very *real value*. Companies and brands alike have realised this and are co-opting our thirst for authenticity to convert engagement to sales.

The ick factor and the halo crowd

Social media has normalised—no, glorified—self-promotion. The most obvious are easy to spot: beach sunsets, gym selfies, overpriced cocktails—we're now comfortable saying 'look at me' with no shame. In social media terms, a post that showcases a way to show off (whether about your prowess in the gym, a lifestyle choice or some other approval-worthy topic) is known as a *flex*. But some flexes are sneakier, hidden beneath (fake) halos, such as the humblebrag, or posts demonstrating moral superiority or spiritual narcissism. For me, these flexes have the ick factor.

The humblebrag is the 'look-at-me' update veiled in fake humility. It comes with statements like 'I don't like to share about my career, but look at this milestone I just hit' or 'Exhausted after another incredible day changing the world', but it translates to 'I'm important, you should clap for me.'

Alongside the humblebrag, here's my extended family of icks:

- **Amateur athletes:** They supply constant Strava updates, plus meal prep and health advice, which is provided like it's a personality type.
- **Crypto-bro prophets:** They disappear when the market crashes, but reappear to drop 'truths' and unsolicited financial advice when it's up.

(continued)

- **Dogmatic diet disciples:** They swear the keto, carnivore, intermittent fasting or whatever diet is trending will *literally* change your life (note: they're likely to be an 'amateur athlete', too).
- **Humble hustlers:** They offer the latest productivity hacks so you can raise six children, write a bestselling novel, get fit and run a company—all at the same time.
- **Relationship gurus:** They're on their third divorce (or are forever single), they obviously know a thing or two about relationships, and they're here to help you know your worth and attract a 'high-value' partner (or thrive without a partner).

At this stage, you may be able to tell that I'm more than a little cynical about advice freely given on social media, whether it's grounded in a genuine desire to help or intended to spruik one's own life choices for applause.

Even more covert are the morally superior: those whose deeply held belief is that they're more virtuous than the rest of us, as they will not-so-subtly remind you. Psychologists Ben Tappin and Ryan McKay define the illusion of moral superiority as a type of cognitive bias, where we overestimate our own moral standing compared to others. Online, this purports itself as perfectly performed moral outrage and self-congratulation, calling out everyone else for not addressing injustices or harm, while simultaneously virtue-signalling. It's the digital equivalent of a soapbox, except when the applause is instant and the algorithms reward this, it encourages even more morally superior behaviour.

The high priest of the halo crowd is the spiritual narcissist: those who bastardise spiritual practices like meditation, acts of service and yoga and convert them into PR stunts for engagement. I raise my hand here as I speak on this from first-person authority—I have been this person.

Perhaps most alarming is the spiritual narcissist's blissful ignorance about the irony of their behaviour. Their broadcasted sunrise vipassana or carefully staged good deed is actually just another moment of self-aggrandising rather than a legitimate form of self-improvement. What started as mindfulness is just *mefulness* in disguise. As Ronald Purser warns in his book *McMindfulness*, spiritual practices like mindfulness—once rooted in the Buddhist philosophy of compassion and awareness—have now been co-opted as personal branding strategies to become part of the capitalist machine. They are no longer catalysts for personal transformation or collective change.

It's easy to identify these behaviours in others but, like throwing rocks in a glass house, we rarely see these in ourselves—and here's why:

- It feels like authenticity: 'I really do meditate.'
- The social media audience, and the algorithms, reward it, so it feels condoned.
- We tell ourselves it's self-expression, not promotion.

Reality check: if you wouldn't share it without the online validation, it's probably not as pure as you think.

There's nothing wrong with celebrating yourself, sharing your milestones and wins, but we need to stop pretending our selfies from the local soup kitchen are purely from the goodness of our heart.

Feeling called out? Skip to the end of this chapter for some brief grounding practices I use for checking the mechanisms around these behaviours.

Authenticity is a sales strategy

Following the rise of social media and influencers, authenticity has become a marketable point of difference—a unique selling point—except it's anything but unique. As Emily Hund explores in her book *The Influencer Industry*, audiences trust individuals over brands, and this shift has created a marketplace where personal authenticity can be leveraged for profit. Recent research by Ebben and Bull explains that influencers 'earn compensation, and even a living, by monetizing "an authentic life," rather than embodying it.' In plain terms, authenticity is no longer just a quality—it is a product, too.

As trust in big consumer brands has eroded over time, our scepticism has turned us to a more relatable source of information: people. We now overwhelmingly look to influencers and content creators for recommendations over traditional brands. The rise of what we now call *influencers* began with bloggers in the early 2000s—the birthplace of the personal brand in the internet age. And these personal brands—who expertly employ authenticity cues—feel more accessible and believable than celebrities. This perceived closeness and sense of attainability makes us feel understood, which amplifies their persuasive power. It's the ultimate selling guise.

Brands took notice and quickly adapted their selling tactics, shifting away from overly edited magazine campaigns and gimmicky corporate messaging and towards *influencer marketing*, borrowing their perceived authenticity. When a product appears in an influencer's life story, it feels like an extension of their identity, not a strategic product placement—except that's exactly what it is. Influencers and brands have colluded, duping us into believing these recommendations are authentic and real. This powerful blend of personal narrative, social proof and emotional resonance drives us to really believe—and to buy.

The commoditisation of authenticity has seen our traditional buying habits collapse. Where once multiple exposures to a compelling marketing campaign were required to influence our behaviour, now we're only one swipe away from making a purchase. And influencers know how to get us there. They use a compelling mix of personalised storytelling, with behind-the-scenes glimpses, personal struggles and detailed routines designed to create intimacy. They address scepticism head-on—'I tried so many products, and I didn't believe this one would work'—to remove doubt and create a sense of honesty. They dissolve barriers to purchase with a simple one-click buy and swipe-up calls to action, and create a sense of scarcity by encouraging fast purchase. Interestingly, we're knowingly and obviously being sold to, but we believe it anyway. Why? Because influencers give all the right *cues* of authenticity: relatability, honesty, transparency, approachability. These cues are designed to mimic trust, but they serve a commercial goal.

In this way, authenticity is now a key sales strategy. The influencer's story arc is the new marketing funnel. Awareness, interest, desire and action can all be collapsed into a single post that's fast and simple: view, engage, swipe, buy—and repeat. For the user, authenticity blurs the line between genuine recommendation and paid promotion. For the influencer, authenticity is a tool to optimise engagement. And for brands? Authenticity is a currency they can use to convert sales.

Embracing the paradox

So, can we really be authentic when using social media? The answer is that it's the wrong question to begin with. Authenticity isn't a static trait; instead, it's in permanent flux—it's a constant negotiation between our inner self and external perception. As Goffman, and many philosophers before him, have argued, we are always performing in some way or another. Being in a state of authenticity is like trying to hold smoke in your hands, as the feeling of internal alignment is constantly adapting to context.

The better question, perhaps, is 'How can I *pretend* well?' Moeller and D'Ambrosio's Daoist lens offers us a way out of the impossibility of being our 'true self' online, instead encouraging an acceptance that identity is always being performed. Authenticity, then, is contextual, and social media is just one of the stages where we perform our identity. To feel aligned when using social media, we need both an acceptance that our behaviour is being curated for an audience, and to gently detach ourselves from our profile self as being representative of the whole. It's just one stage where our identity is performed for an audience—it can still feel like honest expression, but it's not a *definitive* version of you.

In this light, we should strive to use social media from a place of awareness, flexibility and integrity. The 'genuine fake' paradox never disappears, but by understanding it we have the power to navigate it by embracing the masks we wear, but remembering our freedom to change them.

A brief grounding

It can feel overwhelming to keep up appearances online. Here are a few brief grounding practices I use to support more intentional and self-aware social media use.

1. **Take a moment.** Before posting, pause for a moment and ask yourself these questions:
   - Is this performance or self-expression?
   - Does this align with my values and personal code of ethics?
   - Would I actually say this in real life?

If you wouldn't tell your closest friend face-to-face, reconsider posting it.

2. **Enforce the 24-hour rule before purchasing.** Before swiping to buy, ask yourself:

   - Is this something I really need?
   - How will this purchase actually make my life better?

If, after 24 hours, you still feel this is a good purchase and won't make you feel guilty about spending the money impulsively—buy it!

3. **Reclaim 'real-world' time and space.** To feel truly yourself in a world that rewards performance, try returning to environments where your actions aren't shaped by an audience:

   - Spend time in private, non-digital reflection.
   - Do things that bring joy without needing to be seen, and without creating a digital recording of them.
   - Connect with people who knew you before you curated a social media feed.
   - Ask yourself: 'Would I do this if no-one saw it?'

Explore whether how you're choosing to spend your time really aligns with your wants, or if your behaviour is being driven by the expectation it will make for good social content down the track.

PART II

How Your Brain Responds to Social Media

Why does social media feel so compelling? From doomscrolling to compulsive refreshing, the mechanisms behind social media are no mistake. They've been engineered by the world's foremost experts across psychology and behaviour science, marketing and user experience, all to do one thing: to capture and retain your attention.

In this part, we explore the addictive and exploitative architecture of social media platforms. Rather than frame this as a failure of willpower, we'll uncover the very manipulations that keep us hooked.

5

Addictive by Design

The vibration in my back pocket broke my attention away from the conversation. I pulled my phone out—for what must have been the thousandth time that day—and became absorbed by the tiny notification on the screen. 'The *Huffington Post* has tagged you on Instagram,' it read. My heart skipped a beat—this was big. My latest travel-blogging story, on travelling the Maldives on a budget, had gone live, and a platform with over a million readers had just shared it online.

My pulse quickened as I unlocked my phone and tapped the notification immediately. There it was: my article, live for the world to read and judge. The anticipation of validation was unbearable. I needed to know what people thought: would they like it? How many likes would it get? What would people say about it? Oh gosh, what if the comments were negative? How many more followers would I get? Down the rabbit hole I spiralled…

'Alexis, are you even listening to me?'

I was sitting in a café in Europe, on the other side of the world, with an old school friend I hadn't seen in the best part of a decade, and I couldn't focus for my life.

'Oh gosh, I'm sorry,' I hastily responded, my mind split between my phone and the person in front of me.

'All good, I guess,' they coolly responded. Except it wasn't, clearly.

'Anyway,' I shook my head, placing the phone screen-down on the table before continuing, 'you were saying you're planning on heading home?'

I was met with a raised eyebrow, followed by, 'Ah yeah, I just finished telling you that—my grandmother has just passed and my visa is coming to an end anyway, so I might as well move back,' they finished, obviously taken aback that I'd not remembered a single detail they'd just told me.

Internally, I berated myself, mortified I'd just asked the same question twice and so clearly not heard a word they'd said. Why was I like this? Why couldn't I pay attention for more than a second to what people were telling me?

It was clear in that moment that a thread of trust had been broken, my inattentiveness received as uncaring. And in all fairness, could I blame them?

Our presence can be a gift. But I was unable to give it because my attention was being stolen elsewhere. The pings, buzzes and flashes of my phone were too alluring. What they offered felt far more compelling than what was in front of me—*real* human connection. And by allowing myself to succumb to their irresistible temptation, time and time again, I'd unknowingly made myself addicted.

• • •

So far in this book, we've explored how social media rewards and reinforces certain behaviours that encourage strategic self-presentation. But knowing this alone won't necessarily help you shift your digital habits. If you find yourself constantly sharing posts to get validation or doomscrolling for hours before bed, unable to stop, it doesn't mean you're weak-willed. Social media platforms have been engineered this way. Your attention is fundamental to their economy; to keep it, they've employed manipulative hijacking techniques designed to keep you hooked. By understanding the science behind this—the neurochemicals, habit loops and design manipulation—we can begin to reclaim our power over our attention.

Dopamine: Rewards and unpredictable feedback

You're not addicted to your screen because you're lazy, you're addicted to it because your brain is doing what it's designed to do: avoid discomfort and seek reward. It's our natural hardwiring. The problem is that this evolutionary hardwiring—that evolved to support our survival—is now being hijacked by the most powerful dark design features and algorithms in the world.

At the heart of this reward system is a neurochemical called *dopamine*, a tiny molecule that plays a massive role in your motivation. There's a misconception that dopamine is a pleasure chemical, but it's not. Dopamine doesn't make you *feel* good; it makes you *crave* feeling good. And it's this craving that *motivates* you to pursue something that might potentially be rewarding—like social media.

Neurochemicals and social media

Dopamine, oxytocin and endorphins are often confused, but understanding exactly how they're triggered and what they give us as a result is crucial in getting clear on how social media hijacks our brain.

- Dopamine = 'I want it', which fuels the chase for the reward.

(continued)

- Oxytocin = 'I feel secure', which gives us feelings of connection, trust and safety.
- Endorphins (and other opioids) = 'I like this', which gives us the actual pleasure when we get it.

Neurochemical	Myth	Actual function
Dopamine	Pleasure chemical	Motivation, anticipation of reward
Oxytocin	Happiness hormone	Bonding, trust, connection
Endorphins	Released by anything 'fun'	Pain relief, pleasure, euphoria

Understanding these differences helps us see how platforms manipulate anticipation and reward-seeking by triggering the release of dopamine—while not necessarily providing pleasure. It's important to understand how oxytocin and other endorphins work too, as these are all important parts of the human experience—yet social media use doesn't trigger their release. Instead, it keeps us hooked on chasing dopamine, when in actuality we're likely craving oxytocin and endorphins.

Social media doesn't make you happy; it makes you chase what you *think* might make you happy, like validation and social recognition, which is why when we're using social media we feel as if we're constantly in anticipation of something that never actually arrives.

Neuroscientist Kent Berridge first uncovered the addictive nature of dopamine when he discovered that we can become compulsive in the pursuit of a reward even when we're *not* enjoying it. This explains why social media feels compulsive yet unfulfilling. You're not actually addicted to feeling good; you're addicted to chasing the feeling, and that's a very different, never-ending and exhausting loop.

And here's where it gets more complex, and sneakier. Your brain isn't just motivated by the anticipation of a reward; it's constantly recalibrating the gap between your expected reward and what it *actually* gets. Scientists call this the *reward prediction error*.

The reward prediction error helps your brain calibrate perceived expectations against actual outcomes. Here's an example of how this plays out in the context of social media:

1. You post a photo and you expect to get 20 likes (prediction).
2. Instead, you get 150 likes (outcome).
3. There's a big difference between the prediction and the outcome in reality (error) and you think 'Whoa, that was WAY better than expected!'
4. This reaction results in a dopamine spike (a learning signal), which teaches your brain to remember and repeat that behaviour.
5. You post more photos, *motivated* by the potential better-than-predicted reward.

To be crystal clear here, you're not getting a hit of dopamine *because* of the outcome, but because of *how surprising* that outcome was—a critical distinction. If you were to repeat this pattern and receive less likes than expected, this would cause a dopamine drop. This variation then keeps your brain guessing, so it keeps you coming back.

Evolutionarily, your brain is prediction-driven. Humans have survived throughout history in part because of our ability to make accurate predictions, for example:

- If I hunt in the forest, I will find food.
- If I go to the river, I will find water.

- If I hear a rustle in the bushes, there may be a predator.
- If I go to a social gathering, I may meet a suitable partner.

Our ability to accurately predict expected outcomes, and pursue them, has been fundamental to survival. However, in a constantly unpredictable environment—especially a manufactured one, like on social media—our predictive ability has been violated. As a result, our brain flags this uncertainty as important, pumping out dopamine to help us learn and constantly recalibrate the prediction error. But when we're no longer using this predictive ability for basic survival, we end up with a compulsive addiction that distracts us from what's actually important—living your *real* life.

Architected to hijack: Intermittent reinforcement

Through an intricate understanding of how dopamine drives motivation, and how our reward prediction error makes us compulsively recalibrate expectations, social media platform designers have perfectly exploited our natural mental mechanisms to hijack our attention. By manipulating the timing and quality of rewards—likes, comments, views, followers—these platforms keep your reward prediction error high. You never quite know what to expect, so your dopamine system never fully settles. Every single refresh, every scroll and every notification becomes a maybe, and your brain loves to fixate on maybes.

This brings us to the most powerful psychological manipulation tool in history: *intermittent reinforcement.* Coined by psychologist B.F. Skinner, intermittent reinforcement is the highly addictive loop that occurs when we receive rewards randomly—not consistently—which makes us far more likely to repeat behaviours that might lead to those rewards.

Skinner's research—conducted in the mid 20th century, before the arrival of social media—discovered that when animals were rewarded on predictable schedules they quickly learned the pattern of behaviour. For example, a pigeon was consistently rewarded with seeds on every fourth press of a lever. It learned to press the lever four times to get its reward, and stopped pressing the lever when it got its seeds. A predictable pattern led to predictable results, so the animal could correctly predict the outcome. Conversely, when rewards were delivered randomly and inconsistently—sometimes seeds came on the first press of the lever, sometimes the fifth—the unpredictability of the reward meant the pigeon persistently engaged in the behaviour, unsure when or if the seeds would come. It wouldn't stop pressing the lever, even when it got no reward.

Perhaps the most famous example of intermittent reinforcement in action for humans is the advent of the slot machine. Because you never know when the jackpot will come, and you're randomly and inconsistently rewarded with smaller amounts intermittently, you keep on pulling the lever. The chance of reward outweighs the costs, especially for gambling addicts who'll lose more money than they ever stand to gain.

Modern social media platforms employ this exact psychological mechanism, putting the slot machine right in your pocket, all the time. Social media doesn't reward you consistently and predictably—by design. If every time you posted you were guaranteed the same ten likes, by the same ten people, it wouldn't be very exciting, would it? Likewise, if every time you refreshed you saw the same posts by the same few people, you wouldn't be as interested. Instead, you're kept excited and motivated through intermittent rewards—the possibility that the post may go viral, or maybe it will be met with silence—and this keeps you coming back for more. The unpredictability and anticipation of 'maybe' keeps your dopamine system well and truly activated because the uncertainty is a powerful hook.

In this way, your motivational system has been perfectly hijacked: your brain has been trained to not give up, because the next refresh, the next scroll, the next post might provide the reward you're looking for. This makes it nearly impossible to put the phone down or, even when you do, not pick it up again moments later. Except unlike slot machines that belong in casinos, social media is a device in our pocket—the pull of the lever is always within reach.

The gambler's fallacy and the illusion of control

Our brains are meaning-making-machines: while intermittent reinforcement is being used to hijack our dopamine system, we then tell ourselves stories to make sense of these random patterns.

The *gambler's fallacy* is a cognitive trap where we falsely think a random outcome is influenced by a past event. It's what people think when they say slot machines are 'due for a win' or 'running hot'—they are ascribing a false meaning to that random event. It's not logical; it's the brain's way of creating sense in uncertainty. This is relevant for social media, too. If we make a post that performs better than expected, we might conclude it's a result of better hashtags, a great photo or posting at the right time of day, negating the algorithmic forces also at play.

In reality, on social media it's often a combination of reasons that influence the performance of a post. However, when we overestimate our influence on the outcome, this is where the *illusion of control* trips us up. When we get that reward from social media, we start thinking we've cracked the code—we've outsmarted the algorithm. As a result, we stay in the loop, feeding the platform with our time, attention and energy in an attempt to repeat the past result. We keep pulling the lever of chance, thinking we're in control of the outcome.

Here's how this looks across different platforms:

Platform	Trigger	Your prediction	Reward	Gambler's fallacy in action
TikTok	You post a video.	'This one might go viral.'	It might get 200 views...or 2 million.	*'That last one popped off—maybe I've cracked the trend.'* *'If I keep posting, I'll hit again.'*
Instagram	You share a story, reel or photo.	'This will get lots of likes, saves or comments.'	Maybe 5 likes, maybe 500—unpredictable.	*'That post did well—maybe it was the time of day, or the song I used.'* *'Better post again while the algorithm favours me.'*
Email	You refresh your inbox.	'Maybe something important is waiting.'	Sometimes there's nothing. Sometimes it's a new email.	*'If I check just one more time, maybe that reply will be there.'* *'I don't want to miss an opportunity.'*

Like trained pigeons collecting seeds, these platforms are training us to refresh, scroll and post to be—potentially—rewarded. And because we can never accurately predict when or how much we'll be rewarded, we keep coming back for more.

(continued)

The dopamine spike is what keeps you chasing and, as you repeat that loop over and over again, it starts to become second nature. It's a pattern of behaviour we no longer need to think about, so we just repeat it—our brains build a shortcut. This shortcut is called a *habit*, and by the time we've developed a habit we're operating on autopilot.

Forming habit loops

Dopamine doesn't just make you crave; it fundamentally guides your behaviour—teaching your brain what is worth repeating by encoding the reward prediction errors. Every time you experience that better-than-expected reward, your surprise becomes something your brain notes as worth remembering and repeating. The more you repeat the dopamine-fuelled behaviour, the better your brain becomes at automating that process. Eventually, it's no longer consciously thought about, it just becomes something you do. This shortcut is called a habit loop, and it becomes stored in the part of your brain responsible for routine behaviour.

Over the course of the past 20 years, I've formed a multitude of social media habit loops:

- When I'm bored, I scroll Instagram reels.
- When I'm anxious, I continually refresh my email inbox.
- When I've got a hard professional task to complete, I create unnecessary LinkedIn content.
- When I hear my phone ding, I automatically pick it up before I've even thought about it.

As James Clear explains in his book *Atomic Habits*, these are cue-driven loops that form habits. And when what we repeat gets rewarded, it becomes a habit loop (see figure 5.1). Neuroscience research has shown that dopaminergic firing precedes habit formation, especially in cue-triggered contexts. In simple terms, this means your brain starts learning what it anticipates will reward it, and as you continually respond to that cue it becomes an automatic behaviour response. Over time, the dopamine release shifts from the reward to the cue itself—that cue alone is enough to fire the behaviour automatically. Soon enough, your brain stops needing the reward at all, and the cue alone can trigger a response without conscious thought.

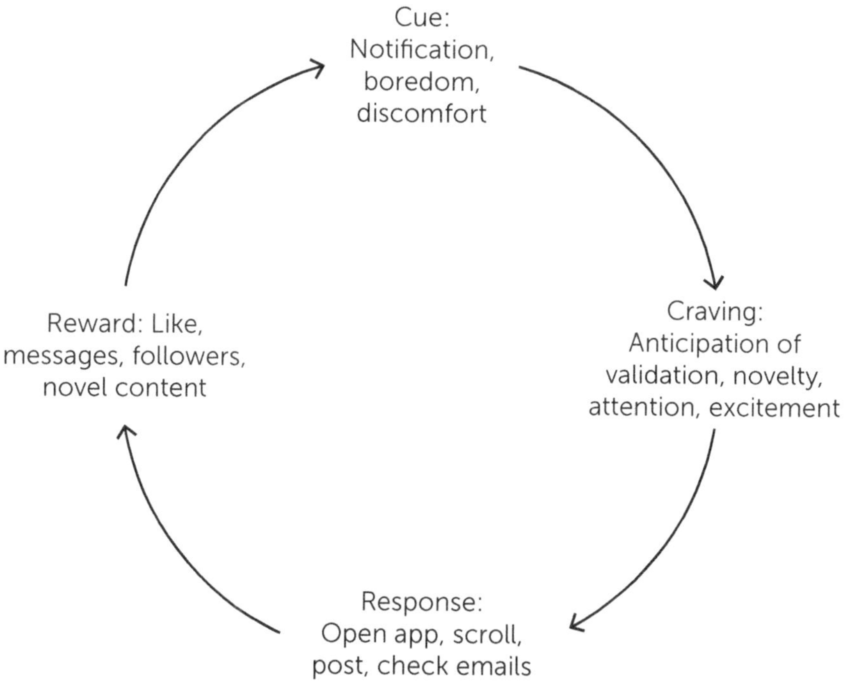

Figure 5.1 The habit loop formed during social media use.

If you've ever felt powerless to doomscrolling, or compelled to constantly check your follower count, you're not alone—and now you know why. I've spent years feeling trapped in compulsive cycles of refreshing my feed to see who's been viewing my Instagram stories and liking my posts, with seemingly no plausible explanation for why this feels so urgent. What was evolutionarily an essential part of our biology has been hijacked to keep us engaged. And when your pleasure-seeking dopamine system meets the powerful and unpredictable reward system of social media, the perfect storm for compulsive behaviour is formed. You're fated to repeat the loop again and again, which your brain hardwires for you. This isn't an accident, it's by design. The result is that you're left chasing rewards that never satisfy your actual needs, in a loop you feel powerless to escape.

But you *can* escape this loop. Once you understand how it works, you can interrupt it for yourself. That's what we'll explore in Chapter 6: how to build your habit loops intentionally so that you can reclaim your attention and curate a digital presence that works for you.

Dark design features that hook

From infinite scroll to pull-to-refresh, read receipts to disappearing content, *dark design features* are the undertow of social media that pull us down into the current of compulsive behaviour. Dark design features are those explicitly built to reduce friction and create increased and prolonged engagement on social media platforms. As a result, these features steer behaviour in ways that benefit the platform more than its user. Posited by technology developers as being innovations that enhance user experience, in reality these features are engineered to make our experience so seamless that it's almost impossible to find our way out of the vortex once we've been sucked in.

Dark design features—invented by some of the world's most brilliant technology developers, psychologists, neuroscientists, behavioural economists and so forth—create such a frictionless social media app experience that we doomscroll endlessly, view for longer and engage well beyond our intention. Even when we know we should put the phone down, we can't. These hooks are deliberate design features—the longer our attention stays engrossed, the more valuable we are to these applications.

These features exploit our innate psychological and behavioural processes and convert them into habit loops or, worse, social media addiction. If you feel the compulsion to pick up your phone every few minutes, it doesn't mean you're weak-willed or unmotivated; in fact, you're behaving exactly how the app developers had hoped.

Combined, these features have created a behavioural ecosystem—a Venus fly trap of sorts that lures us in with entertaining content, then ensnares us through dark features that keep us engaged for longer, lead us to compare more and drive us to seek validation in ways that don't fulfil us. By exploiting our innate psychological and emotional needs, dark design features make social media irresistible. And as our reward system is continuously hijacked, our agency, autonomy and sense of self quietly erodes along with it.

Here are some of the dark design features you're likely using every day—and what they're doing to you.

Infinite scroll and pull-to-refresh

Designed to create a frictionless, endless user experience, the infinite scroll ensures there's no beginning or endpoint to your engagement. While a book, or even an email, has a natural finishing point, the infinite scroll removes this, providing no endpoint to move on to something else. This is problematic for a number of reasons. The first is that it sustains an open-ended reward loop—while you're continuously scrolling, you're rewarded with tiny bursts of dopamine from reel after reel of endless content. You're also continuously open to the influences of the content being absorbed: comparing yourself more to others, absorbing identity cues endlessly and experiencing a near-constant stream of microstresses. The infinite scroll—arguably the most damaging but also the most effective social media engagement tool—keeps you in an always-on exposure loop of reactivity.

The infinite scroll's insidious cousin, the pull-to-refresh feature, is quite literally the pocket slot machine you never asked for. This feature is intermittent reinforcement in action. Every time you pull-to-refresh your screen, you initiate the loop, and the unpredictable nature of the reward keeps you coming back for more. Will you get a funny reel? A horrific update on the latest geopolitical war? A cute cat? A new connection request? Every refresh is a lottery, and our brains love a chance to gamble.

Infinite scroll removes all natural stopping cues, and pull-to-refresh traps you in the constant anticipation of reward—a combination of psychological manipulations that keep you ever-hungry, yet never satiated.

Read receipts and visible social metrics

Our innate need for social acceptance is intensified with dark design features like read receipts, story views and visible social metrics. Recognition, acceptance and belonging are deeply human desires, but on social media they become public and quantifiable. Likes, comments, reshares and follower counts turn social validation into a visible metric of approval. When our lives are constantly on display—through story updates and view counts, showing us exactly who's watching—this visibility can start to feel like relevance. But as we'll explore in Chapter 13, relevance and meaning are not synonymous.

These design features also amplify FOMO (fear of missing out, which we'll come back to in Chapter 7). With constant access to other people's lives, and the knowledge they have access to ours, the pressure to be included, visible and interesting means we feel compelled to not just maintain a social life but to perform it for social media.

This always-on visibility of our social value and belonging is now measurable, and what's measurable is also comparable. This has translated the human need to belong into a socially driven desire to constantly prove our value, which serves to intensify our anxiety and performativity.

Autoplay, up next and algorithmic recommendations

Much like infinite scroll, autoplay, up-next features and algorithmic recommendations create a seamless experience that keeps your attention moving from one piece of content to the next. These reduce the need for you to think autonomously. Rather than asking yourself, 'What do I want to do next?' the algorithm answers the question before you've even finished the thought. It does the thinking *for* you, thus creating a frictionless experience that increases your exposure to more of the same content you've already engaged with; in other words, as the algorithm learns what engages you most, it serves up more of the same. This repetition isn't just shaping what you see but reinforcing a specific perception of the world, and the version of you that emerges within it.

Far from being features of convenience, these features covertly reshape how you see yourself and the world around you by eroding your agency and autonomy.

Stories and disappearing content

Urgency motivates behaviour, and disappearing content heightens scarcity and ephemerality. Vanishing messages, stories and time-limited content intensify the need to check and refresh because we fear we'll miss something socially important. Time-limited content triggers our need to feel included and accepted; if we're missing information, intimate moments or a chance to participate, we feel both uninformed and as if we're missing out.

Gamification, streaks and badges

Gamified social content like streaks, blue ticks and badges are designed to reward regular engagement with a feeling of achievement, status and progress. These features create explicit frameworks for recognition that encourage engagement in particular ways, keeping us coming back for more. Another metric of 'social success', these transform ordinary engagement into a mechanism for social proof. Badges, ticks and streaks have become an identity marker we attach our worth to: 'If I've got a blue tick, I must be more valuable, right?'

Beyond just encouraging our engagement, these features fundamentally reshape how we perceive our relationships and self-worth. While gamified streaks convert relationships into obligations, badges and blue ticks remind us that platform recognition and visibility are markers of value. These features condition us to measure our social desirability, connection and worth differently. Rather than connecting to others purely to meet our innermost belonging needs, we allow social media platforms to dictate this through rewards like streaks and badges. These features have evolved from platform features into visible metrics reflecting our personal success, relevance and importance.

Social media and technology addiction

If your phone feels like an extension of your hand, you might have developed some compulsive habit loops around social media—and it can be a slippery slope. Because social media and technology are so interwoven with modern life, it can be hard to tell when we're using these tools too much. From 'just one more reel' to an hour lost to doomscrolling, our time and attention is increasingly hard to control. So, when does ordinary use turn into something more serious? And when does this become compulsion or dependency?

Because social media and technology addiction doesn't involve 'abusing substances', it's often not taken as seriously. But as contemporary research has uncovered, it can be just as pervasive and destructive. Social media can become a *behavioural addiction*—and it's important to understand for yourself where your usage lies on the continuum. Research is also indicating that social media use can result in *reward deficit disorder*, which is when we experience a reduced ability to feel pleasure in everyday things due to the unrelenting dopamine cycle of social media use.

The following short self-reflection questionnaire is designed to help you understand your social media habits and uncover areas where you might like to focus on rewiring your behaviour. These are not abstract questions; they come directly from validated research scales used to measure social media and internet addiction in young people across the world. By answering them honestly, you can gain clarity on where you sit on the spectrum; from healthy and mindful social media use to something more problematic.

This exercise is not about slapping a label on yourself or feeling guilty or ashamed of your social media use. It's a tool for creating *awareness.*

With awareness we can shine a light on where work is needed. Self-assessments like this give you a chance to pause and ask: 'Am I in control of my technology, or is it controlling me?'

This self-assessment is adapted from clinical tools like the Bergen Social Media Addiction Scale and the Social Media Disorder Scale, and it's written in everyday language so you can quickly see where you stand. Keep your answers and reflections from this self-assessment handy, as we'll be using them in later chapters of the book.

***Disclaimer*:** This is not a clinical diagnosis tool, it is simply an opportunity for mindful reflection. If you feel your social media use is problematic—that is, if it's seriously impacting on your day-to-day functioning, mental health and relationships—I encourage you to speak with a licensed therapist or clinical psychologist so you can receive appropriate support.

Self-assessment: 'Am I addicted to social media?'

Consider each statement and whether it is always, sometimes or never true for your behaviour on social media.

1. I spend a lot of time thinking about social media, even when I'm not online. (It's on my mind when I should be focusing on other things.)
2. I often end up using social media for much longer than I intended. (I log on for a quick check and suddenly an hour or more has passed.)
3. I feel the need to use social media more and more to feel satisfied. (A few minutes isn't enough—I keep craving more scrolling or videos.)

4. I've tried to cut down on my social media or phone use, but I couldn't stick with it. (I plan to limit my time, yet I find myself back on it compulsively.)
5. I feel anxious, restless or irritable when I can't check my phone or social media. (If I go hours without internet access, I get fidgety or experience FOMO.)
6. My social media use sometimes interferes with my responsibilities or relationships. (I've neglected school/work tasks, lost sleep or upset people in my life due to being online.)
7. I sometimes use social media to escape my problems or improve my mood. (When I'm stressed or down, I go online to feel better, even if it's temporary.)
8. Friends or family have expressed concern about the amount of time I'm on my phone. (I may even hide or lie about how much I'm online to avoid arguments.)
9. I feel a constant urge to check notifications immediately. (If my phone pings or I post something, I have to check the likes/comments right away.)

Self-scoring: How many 'sometimes' or 'always' responses did you score? Use the scale below to understand what this might mean about your social media habits.

- 0–1 sometimes or always: Your social media use is under control.
- 2–4 sometimes or always: You may be developing an unhealthy relationship with social media, so consider moderating your use.
- 5+ sometimes or always: You exhibit signs of social media addiction. It might be time to rethink your habits and seek changes for better balance.

6

Attention Management

Your attention is your most precious resource, and right now it's under siege. In Chapter 5, we discussed how platforms hijack your dopamine system and create habit loops, which is why you're constantly checking your devices. In this chapter, we'll explore what that's costing you.

As you can see from the personal example I started with in Chapter 5, the quality of our relationships starts to slide as we become more gripped by our phones than by the people in front of us. During this phase of my life, it wasn't just the quality of my relationships that was in decline—that was just a downstream effect. I had developed the attention span of a goldfish: trapped in the short term, easily distracted and unable to hold my focus on anything for longer than a few minutes. And as my attention continued to fracture, so did my capacity to perform professionally, to recall dates and details easily, to remember important information friends or family had told me, and to solve everyday problems in my life. I was becoming a veritable airhead.

As Johann Hari wrote in his groundbreaking book *Stolen Focus*—which has been pivotal in developing my understanding of addiction—we're experiencing a crisis for attention that extends beyond individual discipline: it's a systematic assault. Make no mistake, this is no mere conspiracy theory. During the research for his book, Hari spoke with a number of expert technology developers, among them Tristan Harris, formerly a design ethicist at Google. Having spent years at Google, Harris explained the very intentional engineering used in technology platforms to fragment our attention. He said, 'If you're not paying for the product, you are the product.' In the attention economy, your fragmented focus is profitable, as you forgo the ability to be present, to think deeply and critically, and you lose creativity and connection, which means you become an easier target for covert influence.

The following table shows how social media and technology platforms have made fragmenting your attention profitable.

Why platforms break your attention	How platforms profit from your attention
Access social media more often and for longer	More time = more exposure to ads
Increases your emotional reactivity	More emotional = higher engagement (likes, shares, reposts, comments)
Generates more data about you	More data = better targeting = increased ad revenue
Reduces your critical thinking	Less thought = easier to influence

The attention economy is multilayered and complex. Platforms don't just want your attention, they want to influence it—and the more you engage, the easier that cycle becomes. Platforms create data points about your habits—the content you like, how you engage and your vulnerabilities—and they use this to fragment your attention further. They push more notifications, content and products specifically curated in the algorithm for you. 'Recommended for you' wasn't just created to personalise your experience, but to commoditise it. Worse, the implications for our attention extend beyond the profitability of these platforms; they unarguably reshape how we see ourselves and our place in the world, too.

Your brain has been designed for depth of thought: to follow a line of enquiry, to connect the dots. It's remarkably capable of solving complex challenges, holding paradoxes and critically appraising information... *when* you give it the time and space to do so. But the problem with our always-on social media culture is that it pushes you into a constant state of hyper-reactivity. Constant pings and vibrations, alerts and pop-up tabs, are continually splintering your attention and training your brain to expect this novelty every few moments. For many of us, this has gone beyond mere moments of distraction; we are permanently *living* distracted.

In her book *Attention Span*, Gloria Mark notes the average person's attention span on a screen is 47 seconds. What could we possibly expect to achieve in less than a minute? What's more, a study by productivity app RescueTime found that mobile device users received on average 63.5 notifications a day, and a significant majority of those notifications came mid-morning and mid-afternoon, often coinciding with work or creative time. This impact has a flow-on effect; research shows how once you've been interrupted by a notification, it sets off a cognitive chain of events, so it can take you 23 minutes or more to re-establish your focus. Let's do a quick calculation here: if an average work day of 8 hours is 480 minutes, and we're interrupted 63.5 times per day, and it takes us roughly 23 minutes to regain focus, that's 1460 minutes... it's no wonder we struggle to get anything done, as there's quite literally not enough hours in the day!

There's an emotional cost to fragmented attention, too. As Cal Newport wrote in *Deep Work*, when sustained attention is required for tasks, we become anxious and stressed about how we're going to maintain this.

Figure 6.1 (overleaf) shows how it looks when we stay stuck in shallow focus as a result of constant distraction.

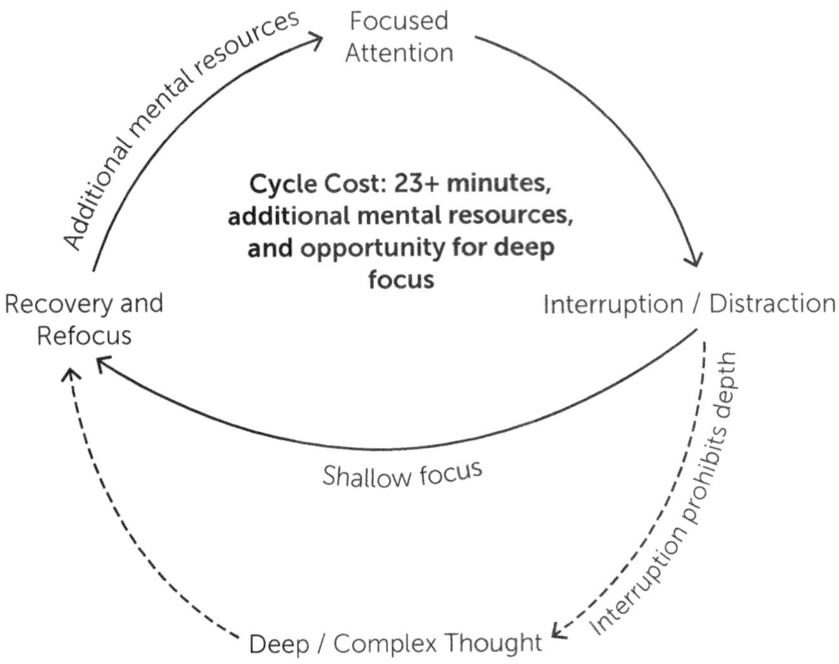

Figure 6.1 Shallow focus reduces our capacity for deep thought.

It's clear: the damage of fragmented attention isn't just in checking the notifications. It lies in the mental residue left behind once our attention is broken, when we experience lingering preoccupation, an inability to access deep cognitive function, and a reduced ability to be creative and in flow states. We're being trapped in reaction and recovery with no ability to go deeper.

Consider the examples of common distractions and their costs shown in the following table, which demonstrates the real-life impacts.

Scenario	Immediate cost	Impact on performance
General interruption—push-alert, notification, phone call	23+ minutes to regain focus	Significant delay in resuming/completing tasks

Scenario	Immediate cost	Impact on performance
Short distraction (2.8 seconds or less)	Doubles error rate	Twice as likely to make mistakes
Switching between complex tasks	Up to 40 per cent loss in productivity	Reduced efficiency and increased errors
App switching	9.5 minutes to return to productive workflow	Decreased productivity and increased fatigue
Self-induced interruption e.g. checking email	Similar negative effects as external interruptions	Slow task completion and poorer quality

The personal cost of distraction

Constant interruptions and distractions aren't just draining your mental energy, they're slowly reshaping how you think, feel and relate to the world—without you even noticing. As the parable of the frog in hot water reminds us, we don't notice these small, incremental shifts happening over time—until we're boiling. No longer is it just your attention that is being fragmented; your very *self* is.

After two decades of chronically shattered attention, I wasn't just less productive and struggling to focus—I was fundamentally different. Less myself. Less grounded. Less present. I could still perform, but I could no longer connect. Where your attention goes determines your priorities—where you spend your time and energy—and this results in the life you live, who you become and, ultimately, the legacy you leave behind. Your mental attention isn't just a resource—it's a mirror for your identity. When it's constantly hijacked and distracted, your sense of self erodes with it.

Having agency over our attention is about more than just our productivity—it's an existential necessity. As Matthew Crawford reminds us in his book *The World Beyond Your Head*, your attention is fundamental to your decision making: when you lose your attention, you lose your agency, too. The loss of your agency inhibits the ability to shape your own reality, on your terms. Crawford conceptually argues that to be able to direct your attention towards something, and hold it there, *is* a form of freedom. It is what enables you to become a coherent self—to make sense of the world and your place in it. Except as social platforms engineer environments designed to coerce and fragment our attention in myriad ways, we experience a slow erosion in our concept of self, and a deeper sense of meaningfulness along with it.

This disconnection from ourselves and from others can leave us feeling emotionally numb and lonely. It's like we've become strangers to ourselves. At least, that was my experience, when I outsourced who I am to the whims of my device.

Rather than align our behaviour with what we value, we're being distracted into a meaningless existence. And as we do so, we feel more frustrated, reactive and desensitised to the emotions of others. The very things that make up our selfhood are in jeopardy. Sherry Turkle explored this in her book *Reclaiming Conversations*: our empathy, emotional regulation and self-reflection are impaired when we're constantly distracted, so the very things that help us relate to ourselves, and others, suffer as a result. And it's the absence of solitude, replaced by the never-ending pings for your attention, that are eroding these qualities. As she said in the book, 'But if we don't have an experience with solitude—and this is often the case today—we start to equate loneliness and solitude. This reflects the impoverishment of our experience. If we don't know the satisfactions of solitude, we only know the panic of loneliness.'

Nowhere is this disconnection more visible or painful than our modern relationships. In a world where we're surrounded by digital connection requests and virtual friends, our fragmented attention has robbed us of the richness of real-world connection. We snub the opportunity to connect in person. We've traded people for devices—and normalised this—but not without emotional fallout.

'Phubbing' is ruining your relationships

When we begin to turn away from the relationships right in front of us, this is more than distraction: we're signalling that these relations matter to us less. This is called *phubbing*: phone snubbing, where we snub people in front of us in exchange for our device. This is exactly what I was doing in the example at the start of Chapter 5.

We've all had the experience of being mid-conversation with a friend, when you hear the gentle 'ding' of a new notification from their phone. You watch as, mid-sentence, their hand slides to their pocket to retrieve it, and their gaze and attention soon follow. You're now met with distracted 'hmms' and nods as they scroll, half-listening. At that moment you might feel a number of things—annoyed, frustrated, taken aback—but one thing is for sure: you'll feel second place to whatever is happening on the screen. A moment of connection has been destroyed. And yet, as modern relationships deteriorate, we seem to accept phubbing as par for the course, despite it being one of the most pervasive and deleterious forces shaping our relationships.

Research has shown that not being fully present when spending time with others erodes the quality of our relationships. When we're phubbed, we feel emotionally dismissed, unimportant and second-best. What's worse, it diminishes our trust, kills intimacy and weakens our emotional connection—all of which take time and investment to build and yet can be destroyed in mere moments. But while phubbing might feel reflexive, you can get a handle on it. That's because it's another habit loop.

Habit loops form when we repeat behaviours often enough that they become automatic (as discussed in Chapter 5). In the same way, phubbing is a habit that develops when we receive a cue that pulls our attention away from the person in front of us, and to our device. It looks like this:

1. Cue: The buzz or ding of a notification.
2. Craving: Anticipation of novelty, connection and validation.
3. Response: You check your phone.
4. Reward: A hit of dopamine from a like, message or connection request.
5. Repercussion: Forgoing the *real* relationship in front of you for the one on your phone.

The irony of this loop is that it's often the social connection and validation we crave that pulls us away from the person in front of us and onto the screen, when we could be experiencing this in person, directly, with presence and undivided attention. Over time, this habit loop makes it harder to give our undivided attention to our real-world relationships, as we fall into the trap of being easily distracted.

Our relationships are a key part of our self-concept, too. We rely on social cues and the perception of others to make sense of our own identity, and so reclaiming our focus in our relationships will not only improve how we relate to others but also how we relate to ourselves. Don't worry, I'm not going to leave you hanging—we'll get to what you can do about this soon.

In the meantime, I want you to think about this: one of the most radical acts of intimacy in the modern world is *presence*, the intentional allocation of our most finite personal resource: our undivided attention. Where are you putting yours?

7

FOMO—Fear of Missing Out

It's Friday night, and I'm snuggled on the couch with a Netflix series queued and ready. I'm tucked into a cosy blanket with a bowl of fresh popcorn in reach—bliss. All week I'd been craving this quiet downtime to catch up on my favourite show after a big week at work. While I waited for my partner to join me, I picked up my phone and absentmindedly opened Instagram. Tapping on the first story highlight, I was suddenly greeted with footage of my friend group at a nearby bar. My chest tightened; a pang of anxiety dropped in my stomach. How come I didn't know about this? Why wasn't I invited? And worse, what was I missing out on? In less than 30 seconds the peace I'd been waiting all week to enjoy had been destroyed. I had FOMO, *bad*.

This is an experience anyone with social media will relate to. Although I had no interest in being at the bar, the lingering feeling of being excluded hurt. And for the rest of the evening, I couldn't shake it. FOMO had hijacked my emotions and my presence, pulling me away from my delightfully quiet night in and throwing me down a hole of unhelpful rumination. Had I done something wrong to not be invited? Maybe they didn't like me anymore? I was spiralling.

FOMO—the *fear of missing out*—is the experience we have when we think other people are having fun experiences in our absence.

Although not conceptually new—the term was coined more than 20 years ago by Patrick McGinnis—our FOMO has been getting worse since the advent of social media and mobile devices.

Why we experience FOMO

FOMO is often confused as a craving for connection and social validation—we want to be part of the crowd. But that's not actually the case. FOMO is a mechanism of avoidance—a feeling we try to move *away* from—and that feeling is the *perception* of being excluded.

Let's unpack this. Certain experiences, like having fun and socialising with friends, draw us *towards* them; they trigger what psychologists call our *approach motivation*. Conversely, FOMO is driven by the fear of social exclusion—it triggers our *avoidance motivation*, which is our natural instinct to *avoid* discomfort.

FOMO is the uncomfortable experience of feeling we're being left out, overlooked or left behind, a feeling so powerful we are compelled to avoid it. This nuance matters, because when we experience FOMO we're not just reacting to our emotions of envy or curiosity, but to a deeper social survival instinct. FOMO is rooted in our evolutionary biology—to belong, to be accepted, to be protected by the tribe—which is why it can be a viscerally painful experience. Researchers Roy Baumeister and Mark Leary found that social exclusion literally triggers our adaptive alarm bells. Think of it this way: FOMO is less about *being* at the party, and more about what it *means* if you weren't invited.

In the digital age, where we can see what every human on earth is doing at practically any moment in time, we can experience a near-constant onslaught of FOMO—even when who we're viewing isn't remotely relevant to us. When we mindlessly scroll the lives of others, from friends to influencers to celebrities, it can feel like we're missing out on more than one night at the bar with our friends—it's as if we're missing an entire world of social opportunities our extended network is enjoying and that we weren't invited to.

For the most part, our FOMO is unwarranted and unhelpful. But if we don't interrogate the feeling when we experience it, even if it arrives involuntarily, we may let it create stories about our social desirability that aren't true ... and we might even begin to believe them. But before we dive deeper into that, let's look at how FOMO works.

The four-stage FOMO model

Akin to the habit loops we explored in Chapters 5 and 6, we experience FOMO as the result of a *cue*—something we see that sets off a chain of emotional and behavioural responses. This cue (or trigger) is then processed in the rational part of your brain—where you try to make sense of the situation. In the case of FOMO, the perception of exclusion feels like a threat—and this results in an emotional reaction.

It's important to note that while FOMO often activates components of our threat detection and stress response system, it's distinctly different from the fight-or-flight response. In this way, FOMO can result in what psychologists Rob Cross and Karen Dillon call chronic *microstress*. Microstress is stress that is ongoing (so it can occur with every scroll of your feed), it feels ambiguous, it's hard to say where it's coming from and is unresolvable, meaning you can't fight, flight or flee your way out—and we're often not even aware of it. Chronic microstress can feel like hundreds of mini rollercoaster dips, which shake up your emotions and leave you feeling mentally and emotionally fatigued—but you're unable to pinpoint why.

There is a way off the rollercoaster, which I'll explain soon, but first it's important to understand how the experience of FOMO impacts your identity (figure 7.1).

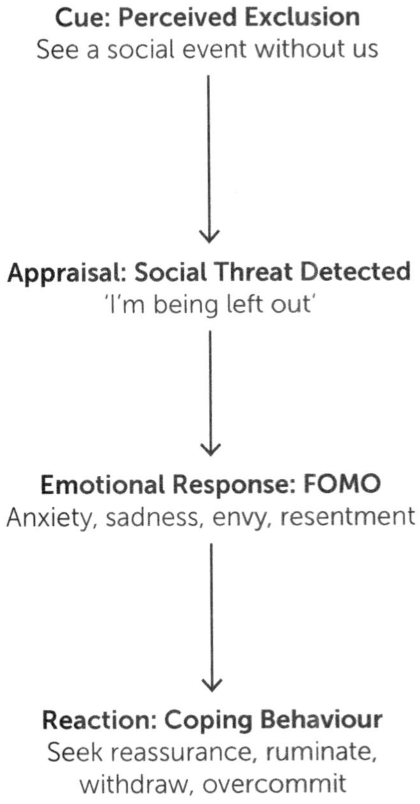

Figure 7.1 The four-stage FOMO model.

How FOMO reshapes your identity

More than just feeling like we're missing out, the regular experience of FOMO can start to reshape what we believe about ourselves. If we're exposed to chronic feelings of FOMO—regular and persistent—we can start to internalise this to mean something about our social desirability, which negatively impacts our self-esteem and self-concept. And this can happen *despite* us actually having real and fulfilling friendships, because we're continually overexposed to FOMO-inducing content on social media.

Repeated exposure to situations that cause FOMO (like social media scrolling) can distort how we see ourselves. This comes in the form of negative self-talk, like 'I'm always left out,' 'I never get invited' and 'I must not be important to them/her/him.' As these narratives infiltrate our thoughts, they colour the lens by which we see ourselves and our relationship to others. The culminating effect? It alters our self-concept.

As discussed in Part I, our identity isn't formed in solitude. It comprises, in part, the perceptions of others—to understand who we are, we need to understand who we are in relation to those around us. And if we believe ourselves to be constantly excluded or unimportant to others, this negatively impacts our sense of belonging and perceived social value. When we truly internalise this, it becomes part of our internal identity narrative and can lead to what researchers call *internalised inferiority*—a belief that we hold less value than others.

FOMO can become a very real downward spiral. Research shows that the experience of FOMO is linked to a lower sense of autonomy, competence and connectedness, which are all core tenets of *self-determination theory* (more on that in Chapter 13). This means we feel less in control of our lives, our self-belief plummets, and we feel disconnected or separate from other people. Over time, this has negative impacts on our wellbeing, making us more anxious and depressed—a sombre picture indeed, but one that's also entirely hopeful... because now that you understand how social media induces FOMO, you have the power to do something about it.

From FOMO to JOMO

What if missing out could actually make us *feel better*? It can. FOMO is rooted in the fear of exclusion, something we naturally try to avoid, but we can intentionally reframe this to be a positive opportunity—something we want to move towards. Enter the *joy of missing out*, or JOMO. When we experience FOMO, we often involve ourselves in social situations we don't actually want to be a part of, just to reassure ourselves of our social desirability and belonging. We'll sit in bars until late at night, catch up with people we don't really like for coffee and go to social gatherings we don't want to be at—not because we truly want to be there, but to avoid the discomfort of what we might miss if we're not. But what if making peace with that very discomfort is how we move forward? What we're actually seeking is inclusion on our terms; we're craving *belonging*.

To truly lean into JOMO, you'll first need to get clear on a few things, including what you value, and the types of relationships and social settings that invigorate you. And you'll also need to be prepared to rewire some of your technology habits that don't serve these needs. To transition from FOMO to JOMO requires you to connect more deeply with yourself. You'll learn practical tools and exercises for this in Part IV, where we dive into reclaiming your agency on social media.

Right now, know this: if you're feeling lonely, socially excluded or like an 'outsider', your social media habits may be playing a bigger part in your self-concept than you realise. As you progress through this book, you'll learn how to peel back the layers of influence and rediscover the brilliant, unique person at your core. You'll also understand how to connect to the world around you in a way that brings you a sense of JOMO and belonging.

8

Algorithmic Curation and Context Collapse

In the second grade, my class was given a project: create a poster about your favourite food. For me that was potatoes (I was an interesting kid). To the school library I went—the encyclopaedia section to be exact—pulling down the thick volume containing everything starting with 'P'. As I flicked through the pages, earnestly looking for potatoes, something that often happened to me occurred: I became utterly sidetracked.

Pablo Picasso, Panda, Peru, Planets. And down the proverbial black hole I went, literally and metaphorically. While far from my original search, I was met with a kaleidoscope of unrelated, fascinating knowledge. And thus began one of my many childhood side-quests: understanding the solar system. A coincidental opportunity born out of chance exposure. (Eventually, I made it to Potato and completed my project—a cardboard poster, from farming strategies to my favourite recipe: Mum's mashed potatoes.)

That accidental curiosity—the kind that blooms from unstructured wandering—gave me wondrous gifts over the years, including niche topics I'd have never found otherwise. But this kind of lateral wandering is harder to do online.

Today, when I type 'potato' into Instagram or TikTok, I'm not met with a wide field of information. Instead, I see a narrow field of what the algorithm thinks I want. Which is what it's been designed to do—conveniently offer me exactly what I've asked in as little time as possible, thus shortcutting the quest and delivering the destination. It remembers my past behaviour, applies filters and indexes popular content. It neatly trims away the randomness. There's no chance of me stumbling across Planetesimal, Plasma or Pluto anymore—that's outside of my curated content bubble.

The algorithm is efficient and effective. It delivers what I've asked for. But in doing so, it strips away all the possibilities of what I *didn't* ask for, removing the opportunity for accidental exploration. And when life only gives you potatoes, your worldview starts to resemble a bland recipe index: efficient and repetitive, but missing the stars.

What is an algorithm?

In short, an *algorithm* is a set of instructions used to solve a problem or make a decision. Think of it a bit like a virtual matchmaker, you tell it what you want and what you like, and its job is to pair you as accurately as possible to things that meet your criteria. And, often unbeknownst to you, it does this by analysing your personal data—what content you spend the most time on, what you search for, how long you watch videos, what those videos are about, who you follow and what you comment on. It then predicts what it thinks you want next, and serves it up in your feed.

Examples of algorithms at work include TikTok's 'For You' page, Instagram's 'Explore' and YouTube's 'Up Next' feed. Even streaming platforms like Netflix and HBO use algorithms to accurately recommend shows and movies you might like, based on your previous viewing habits. What starts as you selecting some general interests for your profile when you join (like travel, nature or sport) becomes a snowball of data over time—tracking every interaction to feed back into the algorithm. Algorithms continuously use these data points to predict, calibrate and nudge your next online interaction. In that way, algorithms are like personal curators: they understand your tastes deeply—*sometimes even before you fully know them yourself.*

Algorithmic doubling down: The reinforcing effect of curated content

Like many of the loops we've discussed so far in this book, your algorithm forms another type of loop—the *identity feedback loop*. The themes of this loop are much the same: the more you repeat something, and the more it becomes internalised, then the more habitual the loop becomes. In this case, the more we feed the algorithm with our curiosity, the more it learns and the more it feeds us similar content.

On the surface, this doesn't seem overly problematic, right? If there are certain things you like, for example rap music, it makes sense that you'd want to see more of that. But as the algorithm doubles down, soon enough your lateral exposure to different kinds of music decreases and your window of curiosity narrows. Over time, this repeated exposure starts to become internalised and rigidly narrow: 'I am someone who only likes rap music.' This may be a seemingly low-bar interest to worry about: after all, what's wrong with only liking rap music? Nothing… until you apply that loop to more complex issues, like politics or religion—things that require both depth and diverse perspectives.

Figure 8.1 shows how the self-perpetuating cycle of the identity feedback loop looks in action:

1. What we view informs the algorithm.
2. What the algorithm serves us shapes our view.
3. What we repeatedly view shapes what we believe.
4. What we believe about us and the world around us is who we become.

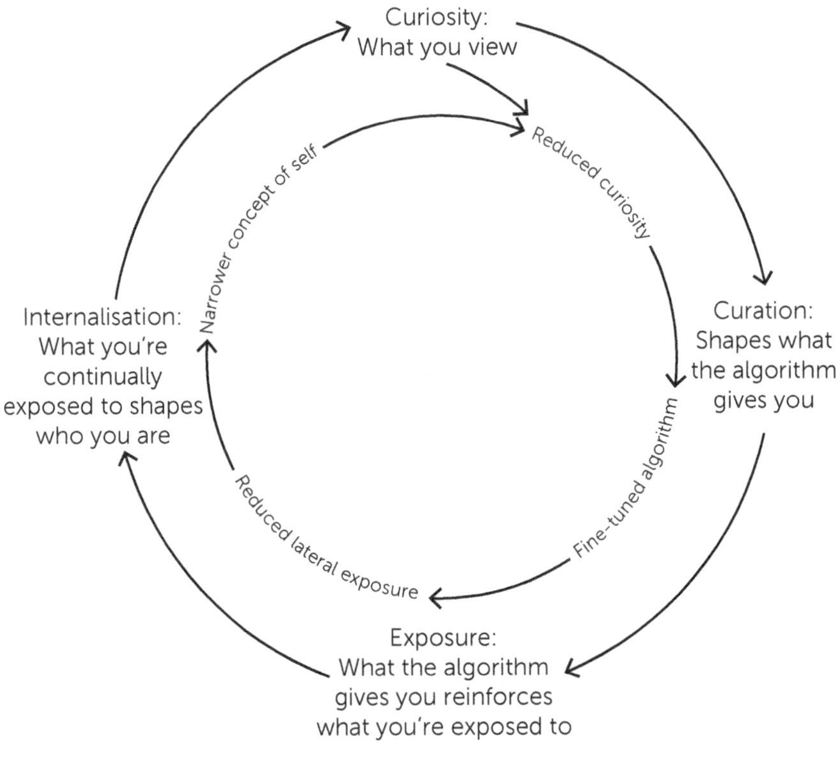

Figure 8.1 The identity feedback loop.

This isn't a secret; algorithms are used in most technologies today to conveniently help us make faster and more accurate decisions by cutting down on searching and thinking time. TikTok's own support website says, 'Once you start interacting on the app, your interactions act as signals that help the recommender systems predict content you're more likely to be interested in … ' A seemingly helpful feature, until it's not.

The result of this continuous cycle of carefully curated content creates what social media researcher Eli Pariser calls a 'filter bubble'—an artificial environment where you become continually exposed to content or news that reinforces your existing beliefs, biases, preferences and worldview, which isolates you from opposing and broader viewpoints, alters your perspective and narrows your frame of reference. And the more the algorithm does its job to fine-tune your feed, the more you slip down the proverbial rabbit hole. Because this is a subtle shift over time, we hardly recognise it. One week we're exploring a new hobby or niche, and within a few weeks that's all the content we see, with follow recommendations and paid advertising that nudge us further down the funnel. But what's sold as convenient hyper-personalisation provides the opposite of personal expansion, and because these choices are being made *for* you—steered by the forces of an invisible algorithm—your autonomy is slowly being undermined.

Researchers have found that the more we're exposed to certain claims or information, the more likely we are to believe it to be true—mistaking repeated exposure for confirmation of truth and validity, even when that information is false. This is called the *illusory truth effect.* When all we are exposed to is the same information, whether it's right or wrong, we start to believe it's true, forgetting there's a world that exists outside that bubble. This has repercussions for our identity, too. As the algorithm reinforces a version of us, a thin slice of the whole, it encourages us to conform to and perform that identity. As a result, our fragmented identity becomes algorithmically reinforced, and we feel increasingly compelled to *become* this performative identity.

Ultimately, this all results in a lesser version of you: a narrower, more rigid view of yourself and the world around you. When we zoom out, this has very real repercussions for our communities and society as a whole. As our opinions, beliefs and identity become reinforced by social media, we slowly close ourselves off to everything outside of that; in fact, we might start to feel there's only *one* way to think, feel and behave. This isolates us from others around us, especially in the real world, as we start to feel less relatable and close our minds to the diversity that surrounds us. As a global community, this puts a strain on our understanding of one another, because we're only exposed to content and people who think, act and feel the way we do. This ends up polarising how we think, causes us to 'other' people who are different from us, and sends us down dark rabbit holes called echo chambers.

Dopamine, scrolling and how the algorithm hijacks your habit loops

You're already familiar with Cue, Craving, Response, Reward—that's the basis of habit formation that we discussed in Chapter 5. But when the habit loop meets the algorithm, the algorithm doesn't just *respond* to your behaviour—it helps shape it. Each time you engage in social media, scrolling, posting, watching or commenting, the algorithm learns what *rewards* you seek, and intermittently rewards you with more. This delivers unpredictable dopamine bursts that not only keep you coming back but also deepen the loop.

The algorithm has an intimate understanding of what hooks you, so it feeds you more, which keeps you scrolling for longer and deepens your exposure to that specific content—continually sharpening its aim (see figure 8.2). When curiosity meets the algorithm, it becomes a dopamine-fuelled loop—what you consume becomes what you expect, crave and ultimately are shaped by.

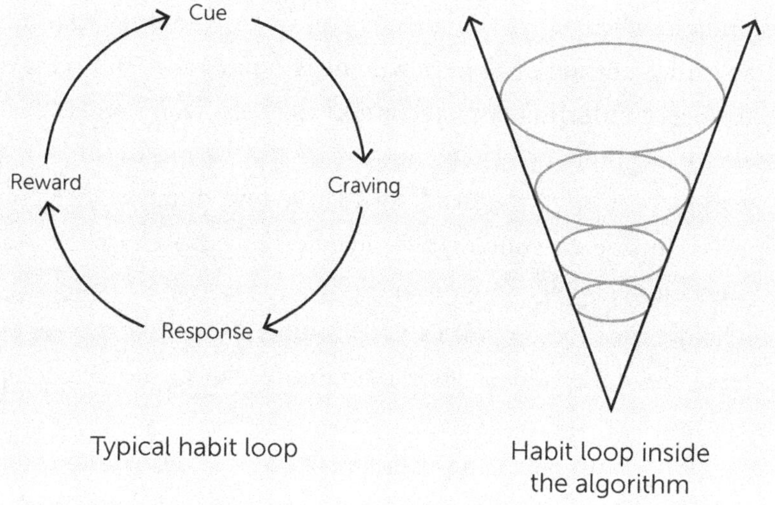

Figure 8.2 How the algorithm hijacks habit loops.

Inside the echo chamber

Beyond the impact on our identity, algorithmically curated (and habit-fuelled) social media feeds have very real social impact repercussions, too. If cat videos are your main social media curiosity, the algorithm feeding you more will feel innocuous. More cute, cuddly and hilarious clips of cats doing cat stuff is unlikely to cause substantial or long-term harm to your identity or worldview. But when the content we absorb matters—like political, religious, social or cultural views—the algorithm amplifying and narrowing our exposure will push you into an echo chamber.

An *echo chamber* is much like the inside of a cave: when you shout into the void, your voice is rebounded back to you. When you're inside an echo chamber, and the algorithm has learned what engages you, the algorithm *reinforces* your exposure to what engages you, rebounding similar beliefs, opinions and perspectives back at you. This creates an environment where what you already feel to be true is compounded, and anything outside of that viewpoint is filtered out and removed. This can feel comforting, as you connect to others who share the same interests, viewpoints or beliefs, but it can also be misleading. In the real world, there are a multitude of diverse and different viewpoints that exist outside of your own—outside the echo chamber—and if you encounter someone with an opposing view, after being in the echo chamber for too long, it can feel jolting. Much like a cave, once you leave the dark void of your rebounding voice, the bright light feels confronting.

Perhaps the most polarising examples of echo chambers came during the COVID-19 pandemic. 'To vax or not to vax' was the question. The internet became a divisive battlefield of righteous—largely ill-informed—opinions about what was right or wrong, from both sides of the debate. And because echo chambers thrive on confirmation, not correction, misinformation and disinformation spread like wildfire. Because algorithms reward engagement, posts that sparked emotional responses and outrage proliferated, leaving common sense perspectives to become not-so-common. Those in the far reaches of the 'for' and 'against' vaccines arguments basically radicalised themselves, forming tight-knit echo chambers where every tidbit of information, whether fact-based or not, became lore.

These echo chambers became increasingly charged, with distrust, uncertainty, fear and personal anecdotes fuelling the algorithm, leaving science-based evidence unable to penetrate and correct the proliferating misinformation and disinformation. In a wildly confronting post-pandemic report, the Centre for Countering Digital Hate found that just 12 individuals, known as 'The Disinformation Dozen', were responsible for nearly two-thirds of all vaccine disinformation across social media during the pandemic. Yet due to the high engagement of this content, which reached millions thanks to the algorithm's love of outrage, the disinformation was able to proliferate across social channels beyond reason.

Disinformation or misinformation?

For clarity, *disinformation* is false information that is created and shared to *deliberately* mislead people. The key difference between disinformation and misinformation is the intent—disinformation is deliberately and maliciously intended. *Misinformation*, on the other hand, lacks this intent and is generally shared from a place of ignorance or provided out of context. In the case of The Disinformation Dozen, their intent was to deliberately undermine the evidence-based science community by creating and sharing information in an attempt to discredit fact and influence the opinions of the wider community.

And don't think you're too smart to fall for the trap. Echo chambers can fool even the most critical of thinkers into narrowing their perspective. As the algorithm functions behind the veil, its subtle nudges may not be perceptible, but they compound over time. Think of it like the frog in boiling water parable from Chapter 6. The broader consequence? Collective fragmentation. As the vaccine debate expanded, we became increasingly separated from the viewpoints of one another, increasingly contained inside invisible walls, increasingly outraged by counterpoints, and further funnelled into groups of only those who think like us and act like us.

This distorts our perception of reality and the world we live in. It robs us of the richness found in diversity of thought, diversity of belief, the opportunity for healthy debate and the enjoyment that comes from experiencing each other fully. What spawns from algorithmic echo chambers and filter bubbles is an inability to hold space for difference, cancel culture and, ultimately, pervasive societal challenges, like radicalisation and hate speech. Rather than bringing us together, echo chambers drive us apart.

And the real shame is that what makes us different from one another is the spice of life—something to enjoy and learn from, not avoid. You wouldn't make a delicious meal with just one spice, so why stay stuck in an echo chamber containing just one narrow viewpoint?

From echo chambers to outrage culture: Algorithms turbocharge the righteous

Cancel culture, and its ideological cousin woke culture, have become toxic on social media, turbocharged by the forces of algorithms and filter bubbles. When our feeds reward moral outrage, ignorant righteousness and virtue signalling, social media becomes a fertile ground for public shaming and call-outs.

Let me be clear here: calling out harmful behaviour appropriately to hold people accountable is an inherently good thing. But when these opportunities are amplified in algorithmic environments, we start prioritising engagement over true understanding. All nuance is lost, and accountability collapses into perverse mob justice. Much like the COVID-19 example earlier in this chapter, research shows that content which sparks emotional outrage—feelings of distrust, anger or rage—spreads faster and wider than emotionally neutral content. In other words, we're addicted to a good drama. And because we engage with it, we get dished up more of it. This is exactly why 'cancellation' moments online exponentially spread, even before we have all the information.

The problem is we often never have all the information or context. Online, moments are reduced to a single tweet, a 30-second reel, a clip or a comment—a snippet torn from its original context, with all its complexity and nuance removed, before being put on trial in front of a global jury. And we're quick to judge, react and define a person's entire identity from that tiny sliver in time. This doesn't seem fair.

Cancel culture is seriously dangerous for two key reasons:

- It's killing free expression—on one side, we're terrified to truly express ourselves out of fear of getting cancelled, so we dilute and self-censor our views and opinions.
- It hardens the ideological divide—on the other side, we hold steadfast to our views and double-down on what we perceive to be righteous viewpoints, placing ourselves on a moral superiority pedestal. *Homogenous ideology* (that is, groups of people who share the same thoughts, beliefs or culture) thrives in cancel culture, where in-group virtue is rewarded, and dissent and difference is punished. This mirrors echo chambers where we're encouraged to double-down on our viewpoints and ignore or blatantly refute contrary opinions, rather than open a space for diverse voices and perspectives.

In cancel culture, we're building walls around our own moral superiority and casting out those who don't agree with us. Ironically, we often feel like we're the open-minded individual when we're cancelling someone else, but in the virtue of doing so we often choose to forgo an opportunity to connect and understand their perspective.

What's worse, when we publicly shame and cancel others, it just makes those walls higher. Research by Dacher Keltner found that someone who is shamed is more likely to experience defensiveness as a response, rather than change their beliefs. This is because shame—like being cancelled—actually triggers a threat response, so we're typically doing more harm (to reinforce what we don't want) than good. And because the algorithms feed on our hunger for outrage, typically the engagement metrics soar—no-one truly wins, but the platforms are profiting at our very public fallout.

Here's four quick tips for resisting cancel culture and echo chambers:

- **Resist knee-jerk outrage:** Hit pause before jumping on the bandwagon, and seek more context, information and additional perspectives.
- **Pursue dialogue over public demolition:** It can feel good—for a moment—to publicly decimate someone, but it's rarely productive. Instead, find an opportunity to engage in dialogue and hold people accountable through constructive conversation that builds bridges, not walls.
- **Diversify your feed:** This isn't the first or last time I'll remind you to push yourself outside the filter bubbles and echo chambers of similar and confirming viewpoints. It's better for you and for society as a whole.
- **Check the performance at the door:** Would you say it to someone's face? If not, don't say it online. Resist the performative urge to use a cancel culture opportunity for notoriety and social clout. Instead, look for how you can truly engage to better understand and empathise with the views of others.

Cancel culture thrives in the algorithmic vortex, sucking us into its spiral of outrage, divisiveness and righteousness. The antidote isn't apathy, but rather deliberate and intentional engagement with those you feel sit on the other side of the fence. We need to resist letting the machine turn our disagreements into digital exile and morally high walls—now more than ever.

Some things should be cancelled, here's how to do it well

The problem isn't that 'cancelling' exists, but that we've allowed it to become unconstructive. Outrage has always been a vehicle for social change, but online it's misfired at individuals for clumsy phrasing, bad jokes and old indiscretions, which are all *distractions* from channelling outrage into the actual systems that cause harm.

When we adjust our aim, public pressure is immensely powerful. Take these notable examples:

- **#MeToo:** A global social movement exposing sexual harassment and assault against women, this sparked real change in societal attitudes, law reforms and support systems around the world.
- **#DeleteUber:** A response from New York City residents in outrage at Uber's perceived undermining of a taxi strike that was taking place in condemnation of a government travel ban on people from Muslim countries to the United States. The result was many users deleting the app and using competitors instead.
- **#FightfortheBight:** An environmental campaign that began in Australia in protest of oil drilling in the Great Australian Bight, a protected and vulnerable marine park. It successfully garnered global support, including from celebrities, and led to the proposed drilling project being withdrawn.

These social media moments drove longstanding and tangible change because they weren't about individual ego and petty point-scoring; instead, they brought people together to surface

(continued)

entrenched injustices and hold political and patriarchal powers to account. They demanded, and succeeded in driving, real systemic change.

So, how do you 'cancel' well?

- **Aim up, not horizontally:** Target systems, corporations, institutions and public figures with real influence and public responsibility to harness social pressure and drive change.
- **Focus on the harm done, not embarrassment:** Call out injustice, discrimination, patterns of abuse and corruption, rather than personal or social slip-ups.
- **Demand change, not exile:** Pair criticism with clear, actionable outcomes, and offer an opportunity for recourse rather than complete condemnation.

Cancel culture shouldn't be a digital guillotine that erases people and their perspectives. Done right, it's an opportunity to educate and encourage others to do better. Outrage is a powerful tool, so let's aim it at power rather than peers, and use it to drive change rather than start witch-hunts.

When all context collapses

While algorithms shape *what you see*, it's equally important to understand how social media shapes *who sees you*. Our identity is complex and fluid, and it depends on the context: for example, there's the professional you; the version your friends know; the one only your partner sees; the family you; and myriad more versions of 'you' depending on the situation. In varying contexts, we naturally code switch between these roles ... except on social media, where all of these audiences collapse into one.

This is what scholars Alice Marwick and danah boyd have coined *context collapse*: the convergence of these previously different and detached audiences in our network all being rolled into one. On social media, everything you post is seen by everyone — the audience boundaries are blurred. Aunt Marge, your crush and your new boss know exactly what you did on Saturday night, which is not ideal. Context collapse is inevitable on social media, unless we're carefully vetting who we allow to befriend and follow us and on what profiles — which can raise conflict itself, because it's no fun when Aunt Marge grills you at a family lunch about why you won't accept her friend request on Facebook.

Context collapse changes how you behave on social media. Researchers have uncovered that when multiple audiences collide, we begin to police our own presence more carefully, self-censoring what we post into a diluted version of who we are. You're trying to balance the expectations of many, while simultaneously being you; you might second-guess posting a picture, neutralise your opinions or change how it's captioned so the post is more palatable for the wide and diverse audience. What's more, Marwick and boyd found that this constant self-filtering can cause a real mental and emotional drain, as self-expression feels more like risk management.

The work of philosophers Hans-Georg Moeller and Paul D'Ambrosio offers a deeper lens here. They suggest our profile self — our persistent, curated online identity, which was introduced in Chapter 1 — is not just a reflection of who we are, but a performance specifically optimised for visibility and engagement across these collapsing contexts. The profile self is a simplistic version of you that's always public and always performing. It's *shaped* specifically for context collapse because it is designed to be performable across every context. The trouble is, it flattens the complexity of our real self into a fragment of the whole, causing us identity strain.

Context collapse makes us feel like we're on stage performing for everyone, all at once, with no script. When we share something vulnerable—a less polished and more revealing side—we experience what author Brené Brown calls a *vulnerability hangover*: the residual anxiety of being exposed after self-disclosure in front of a large, mixed audience. But in the profile self era, this exposure isn't a side-effect of social media—it's actually a key feature. Even our vulnerability has become content, folding itself into the performance, from backstage to carefully curated front. And as we're rewarded for the fragments of self we project—those palatable, and arguably vanilla fragments that are suitable for the masses—we continue to censor and splinter the whole self.

PART III
The Social Web

In this part, our focus shifts outwards—from the self to our connection with others. We examine how social media shapes how we relate, communicate and belong.

It explores pseudo-connection, parasocial relationships, the illusion of intimacy and credibility. How is it we're more connected than ever, yet loneliness and mental health challenges remain on the rise?

9

Genuine Connection versus Pseudo-Connection

I lay sprawled across the couch, still in my work clothes. Another long day in the office followed by a busier than usual commute home had left me foul-tempered and tired. I'd missed my usual gym class and, frustrated, cancelled last minute on drinks with my friends. Instead, I was doomscrolling on Instagram, with my phone screen a mere few inches from my face while YouTube blared on the television in the background; some new protocol about resetting your sleep habits—just another thing I should get on top of. Sucked down into the vortex of mind-numbing reels, video after video after video, I descended further into the fog of the algorithm. Scrolling back to the top of my feed, I noticed a new story from one of my friends—the ones I was supposed to be at drinks with. I tapped his story and there on my tiny screen I saw my friends laughing and clinking glasses to cheers the end of the week. The pang of missing out hit like a gut punch, twisting my frustration into something worse... self-pity. There I was, home alone on a Friday night with nothing to do but scroll. But this mood was entirely of my making. I had a choice: leave a tough day behind me and find solace in connection with people, or isolate myself and doomscroll social media—which inevitably made me feel worse. My frustration became amplified. Not only had my day been crap, but I'd chosen to make it worse by not giving myself what I really needed: human connection.

In such moments, when life feels stressful or frustrating, often our first instinct is to self-isolate and avoid people. And while in some instances this is needed, oftentimes it's robbing us of a circuit breaker—a chance to reset our mood. Instead of choosing connection, we turn to social media or video streaming—even when we intuitively know better—which only exacerbates our mood and makes us feel further isolated and lonely.

We are hardwired for connection; in fact, as innately social creatures, our survival depends on it. But in the digital age our relationships have shifted, from people we meet socially in our communities to now include online connections and followers we've likely never met. This shift is not inherently a bad thing. Today, we can expand our network well beyond our immediate geography, which provides us with an opportunity to connect and belong in 'tribes' far from those in our direct physical surroundings. However, when we *replace* real connection with online ones, we forgo the nourishment this brings—and without this fundamental human need, we suffer.

In a landmark study, psychology and neuroscience professor Dr Julianne Holt-Lunstad and her team analysed data from over 300 000 people to understand the role social connection plays in our wellbeing. Their findings were remarkable. In short: regardless of your age, gender and general health status, social connection was the biggest predictor of living longer. In fact, the study equated a lack of social connection to be *as harmful* as smoking 15 cigarettes a day. Social connection was even a more powerful indicator of life expectancy than exercise and obesity.

These findings have reshaped our understanding of human health, and yet despite it, we still find ourselves in what experts are calling a *loneliness epidemic*. And while in previous eras loneliness was normally a result of social isolation—like when we age and find ourselves living alone—today, loneliness is as pervasive for younger generations as it is for older people.

Paradoxically, we're more connected than ever before, yet we feel lonelier.

The US Surgeon General Vivek Murthy—whose role in simple terms is the nation's 'head doctor'—concluded his role in 2024 with a parting prescription: *choose community*. Even the world's best doctors now recognise social connection as the most important factor contributing to human health in our modern world.

The benefits of social connection are much more than it being a mechanism for avoiding isolation and loneliness. Beyond the basic need for connection as a means to survive, we have an innate need to feel like we belong—like we're part of a tribe, a community. Belonging makes us feel seen, heard and valued by those around us. It reminds us we have a vital place in the world that only we can fill. And when we feel this way, we experience less stress, we become more resilient, and our wellbeing improves.

The biological imperative for social connection is unquestionable, but as we continue to barrel towards a future laden with social media, technology and AI-everything, is the promise of online community delivering social connection or is it undermining our social needs? The short answer: it's doing both.

Perhaps a more important question is this: How might we use social media in a way that builds bridges and bonds to community and connection, rather than replacing it with screentime and keyboards?

Note: This chapter focuses on social connections in the context of friendships and acquaintances—some of the most undervalued yet determinative relationships that impact our health and wellbeing.

Is social media making us lonelier?

Social media can result in both connection and loneliness—the chicken and egg dilemma. Early research on the impact of social media was quick to point to it as a *cause* of loneliness and disconnection, but this explanation over-simplifies what is a deeply complex and nuanced challenge. Social media use can be *both* a symptom of social disconnection and loneliness, and the cause. Feeling disconnected and lonely in everyday life might be a reason you turn to social media in the first place. It can be a vital lifeline out of loneliness, extending a bridge to people and community. But here's the simple truth: using social media with the expectation of it meeting *all* your connection needs is a mistake.

When we're feeling lonely, what we're missing is the feeling of connection. We're craving quality interactions with *people.* And this doesn't need to be a high volume of interactions, but rather a connection on our terms that feels meaningful to us. You've probably heard the saying, 'feeling lonely in a room full of people'; this is exactly what high-volume, low-quality interactions give us. Social media offers plenty of low-effort interactions: comments, quick messages, story views and likes. But this passivity—viewing the lives of others without really participating in them—doesn't fulfil our social needs to their full extent. And, sometimes, it can leave us feeling worse.

We all crave being known but are increasingly uncomfortable with the vulnerability of being truly seen. This is because social media has provided us with an easy out: low-bar, low-risk connection that requires little effort on our behalf. We're in touch, without human touch. Always there, without really being there. Social media offers *pseudo-connection*: the illusion of connection, without any of the juicy parts. This passive engagement allows us to avoid the sometimes messy, sometimes uncomfortable parts of real relationships; in other words, the human parts. But this pseudo-connection is a poorly performed cosplay of human relationships, because when we're too exposed to the passive, we're not actually participating in our relationships.

This is a two-part problem: the first part is that social media is changing how we conduct our relationships, making them easy to the point of passivity; the second part lies in the actual content we consume, and then internalise, on social media.

What started as social networks have now traversed into social media. 'Media', by definition, is a mass form of *communication*, not connection. It exists to broadcast, publish, inform and influence. The 'social' part is a misnomer at best. And although its dialogue is seemingly two-way, it falls short of satiating our deeper connection needs. We were promised global unified human connection, but what we got was a coalescence of algorithmically driven content, hyper-personalised to drive engagement and exploit our vulnerabilities to sell us products. And it's the messages we constantly and continuously receive on social media that drive us further out of touch with one another than ever before.

Do we choose pseudo-connection over real relationships simply because it's conveniently at our fingertips? That's part of the reason. But the undercurrent of the messaging we receive through social media is the modern capitalist throughline that getting and staying ahead is important above all else. That being fastest on the hamster wheel is superior to taking the slow route in good company.

Scroll for just a minute in your recommended reels and pop psychology will offer you a hundred ways to be more productive, hustle harder, optimise better and boundary-set more firmly, which are all messages pointing to rugged independence as a mark of individual success. We're simultaneously being told to do more, be more and achieve more, while divorcing ourselves from connection and community.

Figure 9.1 (overleaf) shows how social media can reinforce loneliness and social disconnection when it becomes our sole form of connection.

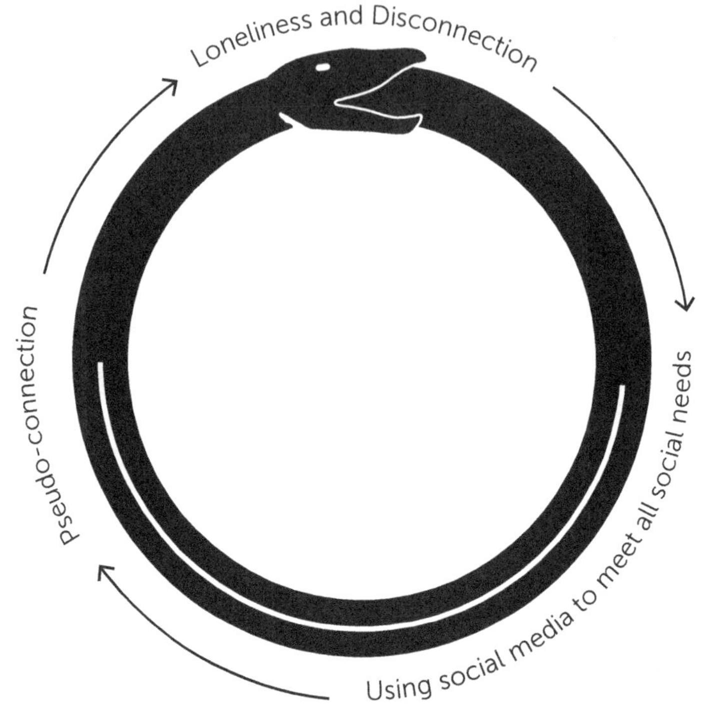

Figure 9.1 The reinforcing cycle of social media use, pseudo-connection and disconnection.

The modern centralisation of individual needs isn't a net negative on the whole—indeed, when we know ourselves deeply, we can also better understand our connection needs—but if we continue to choose the five-inch screen in front of us and call it *being social*, we're denying our most innate human needs of connection and belonging. And these can only be found in the presence and understanding of the community.

Social media alone is *not* the antidote to feeling lonely, isolated and disconnected. But it can be a great enabler to connect—*one* tool of many in your toolbelt. Understanding how it can be used to form connections and integrate and supplement your real-world relationships is vital to it being a positive part of your broader social network.

The promise and perils of online community

As a teenager, I developed a healthy obsession with music. Metalcore music, to be exact—the era where the 'emo kid' subculture was born. I was only too eager to cast aside my beautiful wardrobe of colourful outfits for an all-black ensemble. Like all teenagers, I was going through a period of identity formation and wanted to explore the multitude of options of who I could be. While most of my school friends wanted to shop at the mall, blast Katy Perry and have sleepovers, I wanted to listen to heavy music, learn to play the drums—to my parents' dismay—and go to gigs where singers screamed incessantly and guitar riffs all but exploded your eardrums. It was a pretty niche subculture for the regional Australian town I grew up in, and it was a period in my young life when I had to recalibrate where I belonged.

Thankfully, it coincided with the dawn of MySpace: one of the original social networks, a place where I found an outlet for this self-expression and an opportunity to connect with other 'emo kids'. I spent hours curating my online profile: selecting my Top Friends list, choosing the perfect background song and taking cringey selfies showcasing my full face fringe on a digital camera. It was an opportunity to safely try on this new identity, express it through the form of a curated profile and feel part of a community not available to me in the real world. Due to the technological restrictions of the platform—there were no reels, real-time story updates or even instant messaging—it didn't entirely fill my need for connection, but it provided a bridge to find people who could. MySpace enabled me to connect with friends outside my local town and form the foundations of bonds that could then be deepened in person when we met at gigs, artist signings and battle-of-the-band competitions. It created seedlings for relationships that would grow and flourish when tended to *in real life*. It was an incredible gift—one only a social network could deliver.

This is an experience millions of people can relate to on social media, particularly those with niche interests, who are part of a minority (for example, LGBTQIA+) or have experienced challenges and trauma that aren't commonplace, to name just a few. Social media provides a point of connection, an outlet and a place to belong when your real-world surroundings don't feel like they offer this. And research shows this can have a profound positive impact on your life, from improving your self-empowerment and confidence, to learning new skills from global experts and finding emotional and mental support. Social media can build bridges to people, community and subcultures like nothing had before.

Social media has even resulted in saving and changing lives. In some incredible cases, organ donors have been found through online networks in the absence of a local donor, or long-lost siblings and family have been reunited where traditional records had failed. Social media has even made it possible to meet your significant other on the other side of the world—what had previously seemed impossible became possible. Yet, alongside its radical potential, using social media comes with undeniable risks.

Although social media can provide connection, it cannot fully replace the physiological benefits that real-world closeness to others gives us. When we connect person-to-person, our brains produce a neurotransmitter and hormone called oxytocin. Oxytocin is released in response to sensory cues like physical touch, eye contact, shared experiences, and acts of affection and trust. Typically dubbed the 'bonding hormone', oxytocin is foundational to our stress regulation and emotional resilience, and it helps us build feelings of closeness to others. In fact, oxytocin is a natural analgesic: when it's released in our bodies, it can actually reduce physical pain. Unlike dopamine—which we *can* experience via our online relationships—oxytocin is linked to in-person connection. This is why we can feel stimulated and affirmed by our online relationships, but we don't experience deeper the nervous system regulation and relief oxytocin provides. So, while social media can provide a bridge to connection, it can't simulate the closeness and presence required to release oxytocin—and our bodies know the difference.

What's more, our relationships aren't just about what others give us. They are foundational to our sense of identity; they're also rich with the opportunity to feel a sense of purpose and contribution, and to serve an important role in the lives of others. Being of service to others, such as being a loving and caring friend, family member, partner and community member, gives us a sense of meaningfulness and value. When we're contributing to others, we feel good about ourselves. Researchers call this the 'helper's high'—the feeling of joy, gratitude and calm we feel as a result of helping and contributing to others. This is because this type of connection releases dopamine *and* oxytocin into our system, proving that when we give our time, presence, attention and contribution to others, we also receive.

Social media is fundamentally shifting how we view social connection, and we're at risk of becoming over-reliant on its role in our lives without the balance and integration of these real-world relationships.

Typology of social connection

I'll never forget the adjustment from over 100 notifications a day to dead silence when I first quit social media. The contrast was shocking, and the suddenness in which I felt forgotten was unsettling. But what I slowly came to realise was the space and clarity that silence brought me. No longer was I beholden to myriad group chats with people I was loosely affiliated with. I realised I neither cared what they were doing, nor missed the company. I had been maintaining a huge volume of connections with little to no thought about whether they were adding any value to my life. I had prioritised quantity over depth, and I was exhausted.

Social connection is fundamental to our human experience, but not all connections are created equal. Understanding the types of social connections that nourish and sustain us helps us make better decisions about where and with whom we spend our time and energy—both online and offline.

Everyone's social needs are different. Some of us thrive with larger, extended networks, while others prefer smaller circles. Some relationships expand our thinking, expose us to new ideas and build community, while others help us to feel grounded and secure—and if we're lucky, we have relationships that do both. But one need we all share is the desire to be known, to feel accepted and to feel safe in the company of others: we need to feel that we *belong*. And this doesn't come from shallow or passive forms of connection, whether online or offline.

Recent data shows that the average person has fewer deep connections now than we did 30 years ago, which some researchers are calling the *friendship recession*. Undoubtedly, modern life presents challenges for making and maintaining friendships—from the cost of living to changes in how we work—but it also speaks to our increasingly individualistic tendencies, too. We're prioritising solitude more and more; as social media allows us to maintain loose connections, we're accepting this as being good enough. But depth and active participation are both core tenets in relationships that help us feel we belong—and both require real-world effort.

Despite craving depth, we're often over-reliant on passive and superficial connection. Social scientist Robert Putnam popularised two distinct types of social capital in his book *Bowling Alone*: bonding and bridging. *Bonding* is the close, intimate ties we form with other people like family, partners, close colleagues and best friends, while *bridging* is the relationships we have in our wider network—the kind of relationships that traverse social groups and connect us to diverse perspectives and groups. In simple terms: we need deep connections as well as a wide, broad network.

How we interact both online and off is also part of this equation—specifically, whether our interactions are passive or active. *Active connection* is when we're engaged, maintaining our relationships through spending time with our friends and messaging, calling and supporting them. This type of connection leads to a deeper bond with others. Conversely, *passive connection*—whether offline or online, like scrolling, liking and viewing stories, or simply interacting out of convenience or ease of opportunity—results in us feeling less connected to others.

Balanced social connection includes all the above—bridges and bonds that are both active and passive—but to sustain our social needs over time we need to consciously keep the equation in balance.

There's no magic number of each connection you should have, but if you're experiencing feelings of loneliness and disconnection, there's a good chance you're not getting enough of the deep connections. Having too many loose and familiar connections might leave you feeling like you know a lot of people, but those relationships are likely to be shallow and unfulfilling.

These four terms can be used to describe the different kinds of connections:

- **Loose connections (bridges, passive):** Surface-level interactions with loose acquaintances in your social network. It's those people you 'see around' or know of, but don't know deeply. It's acknowledgement without emotional depth.
- **Familiar connections (bridges, active):** You might interact occasionally or even a lot, have a chat in person or share a message online, or you're part of overlapping circles either online or off. These connections you feel familiar with but not overly close to. They can open the door to broader networks and diverse perspectives when invested in.
- **Close connections (bonds, both passive and active):** There is reciprocal care, active engagement and a genuine desire to maintain a bond. This might include regular messaging, video calls or catching up in person. You're able to share real things and have a trusting and reliable relationship.
- **Deep connections (bonds, active):** Where true understanding and belonging lies. These are the people who see you, make you feel safe and value you. These relationships are built over time and require trust, commitment, sustained contact and often in-person interaction — at least initially. These meaningful relationships are often rich with shared experiences that foster closeness and genuine care.

Figure 9.2 shows these four types of connections in a different way.

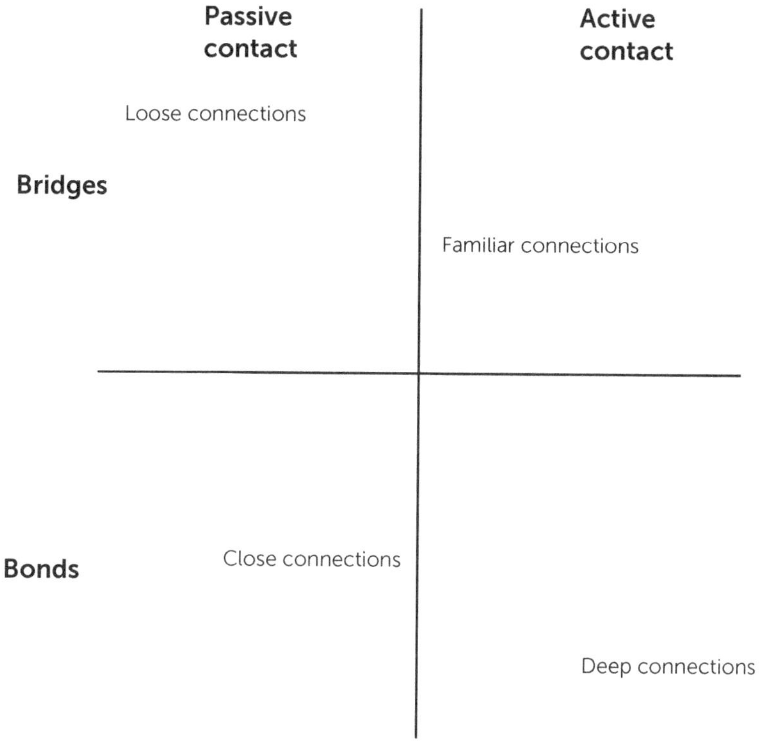

Figure 9.2 The basic typology of social connections.

Online environments are a great place to sustain already strong bonds with others when relationship challenges like geography are a factor, and they provide a fantastic space to initiate connections with new people. But ultimately, to truly feel a sense of belonging, we need to actively invest time and energy into our relationships to take them from loose to deep connections.

Balancing our social connection needs: The connection audit

How do we nourish ourselves with social connections that truly meet our needs for deep connection and belonging? By ensuring we're investing in the types of connections we need most. Now that we understand that bonds with active participation create deeper connections, we're able to prioritise nurturing these relationships, and allow reasonable numbers of the others to varying extents in our network.

Let's start with a connection audit, so you can get clear on what types of relationships you have, and what you're missing.

Awareness: Understanding the types of connections you have.

1. Reflect on your online relationships and ask:

- Am I connecting or consuming?
- Am I mostly actively engaged (messages, chats, video calls) or passively engaged (lurking, liking, watching)?

2. Does this connection feel positive (energising, fulfilling) or negative (envious, hollow)?

For passive, negative connections, consider if these are connections you want to continue having or ones that should be removed from your life/feed.

Balance: Am I getting a good variety of different connections?

1. Do I feel fulfilled with how many in-person and online relationships I have? Also, is there a balance of deep connections through to loose connections?

2. Am I using online spaces to initiate and sustain my connections, but not to replace them?
3. Are there any types of connections I feel like I am missing?

There's no perfect balance here; we're all individuals with different social needs, but you should feel that you have both deep and loose connections online and offline.

Perhaps you feel like you have a lot of loose connections offline? How might you shift your focus to building closer, deeper connections? Or perhaps you feel there's people you know online who you'd like to get to know more deeply—how might you initiate that relationship offline?

Boundaries: Maintaining balanced connection across online and offline environments.

1. Designate offline time for solitude, family time, and in-person meet ups. This might include transitioning connections made online into offline environments safely, or spending time with an acquaintance to deepen a relationship.
2. Set up periods for 'deep social time', including nurturing both online and offline relationships with active engagement. For example, Facetime a friend who doesn't live close, rather than just liking their content, or have screen-free time with a close friend in real life without social media distraction.

Boundaries are a way of recalibrating to get more of what you actually need, rather than just more of the same. Key indicators that you might need to enforce boundaries and shift your connection habits are if you're feeling unfulfilled or disconnected from others—this applies to online and offline connections.

(continued)

Integrate and sustain: Keeping connection alive across your network.

1. Let digital connections lead to real-world relationships and utilise social media to maintain connections made in person when you're separated. Look for moments when passive participation can lead to active participation, for example if a friend sends you a meme, it may remind you to text them for a coffee.
2. Create rituals of genuine presence. Whether online or offline, look for ways to create deeper bonds through active engagement, such as video calls over text messages, and meetups over online forums.

Connection in the digital age is complicated, but when used strategically social media can act as a bridge to sustain and deepen the connections in our lives. Online connection can drive empowerment and discovery, but it can't entirely replace the closeness and depth we experience in our offline relationships, which is why it should be integrated to meet our social needs but not replace them.

We all experience a need for connection. When we notice the signs of loneliness and disconnection creeping in, taking an intentional and balanced approach to meeting our connection needs creates a sense of belonging in our offline and online world (see figure 9.3).

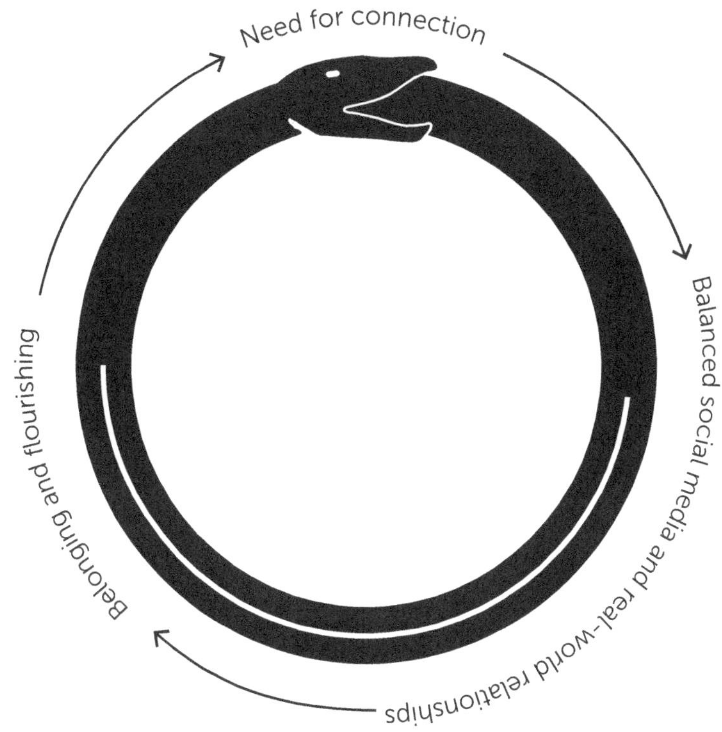

Figure 9.3 How social media *can* reinforce belonging and flourishing.

10

Parasocial Relationships

'I cannot believe they broke up!' my friend exclaimed over brunch.

'I know!' remarked another.

'She's way too good for him anyway, he was just riding on her brand,' I added, sipping my coffee. My partner listened intently, patiently trying to keep up, as the details of the fallout were discussed.

After another five minutes of feverish exchange between us, he interjected, 'Wait, what—these are influencers? You're talking like you know them!' We were silenced. And if looks could kill, they would have—offence was written all over our faces.

'Well, we kind of do ... ' said my friend, her voice dripping with annoyance.

'You literally do not know these people,' he said. 'Why do you think your opinion on their dating lives even matters?' He was clearly equally perplexed and irritated that we'd just wasted our precious time discussing what he felt to be inane.

We may have been offended at the time, but he was right. Here we were, a group of friends who caught up once in a blue moon for brunch, and we were wasting our precious time gossiping about influencers who didn't know we existed. But we *knew* them ... well, kind of. We saw every minute of their lives and their relationship unfold intimately on Instagram. We knew what pyjamas they slept in, where they liked to get coffee in LA, their favourite bagel flavour, what the inside of their home looked like and their pets' names. That's more than some of my actual friends knew about me, so if I didn't *know* them, then what was this?

We had developed what psychologists call a *parasocial relationship*: a one-sided bond that forms towards someone we don't actually know. These types of relationships aren't new. Originally proposed back in the 50s by researchers Donald Horton and Richard Wohl, a parasocial relationship is a one-sided emotional connection people develop towards celebrities and media figures. Fast-forward 70 years and social media has amplified this exponentially, because now we get to see *everything*. Historically, we fell in love with the 'public' version of celebrities—the one on screens, stages and magazine covers. But with social media, we now see every moment lived in real time, giving us constant, intimate access to the lives of our favourite celebrities, sporting heroes and influencers, which amplifies the feelings that 'we know them'. Add to this the ability to engage with their content—liking, commenting and resharing—and the illusion of intimacy is formed.

And it's not just the megastars we form these bonds with: parasocial relationships can occur with public figures with fan bases of any size, from well-known influencers, celebrities, movie stars and sportspeople through to micro-influencers and niche creators. But like all connections formed online, balance is key.

The hidden costs and surprising benefits of parasocial relationships

Parasocial relationships are not only a normal part of social media—they're *inevitable*. Although they're often associated with celebrity obsession or extreme fandoms, parasocial relationships aren't inherently bad or weird but a normal byproduct of relating to people we're continually exposed to in a non-reciprocal way. Interestingly, there's gender discrepancy in how parasocial relationships are perceived too: when women form them, it's often categorised as 'fangirling' (such as the One Direction mania), but when men form them, it's often normalised, even celebrated (sporting teams and YouTubers are common examples).

Parasocial relationships actually play an important role in our self-concept. This is especially true for teenagers when they are forming their identity. In Chapter 1, we covered how our self-concept and identity isn't developed in isolation from others; instead, we develop our sense of who we are both with and alongside others. We *rely* on others to understand ourselves, and parasocial relationships are a reflection of our self-concept. For example, we're drawn to certain celebrities, influencers or sporting heroes who role-model traits, values, achievements or lifestyles we admire. The more we identify with them, the more motivated we become to feel affiliated with them. And this need for affiliation drives our behaviour via influence. We might find ourselves dressing in a certain way, listening to a certain music genre, buying specific products or brands, and even associating with others who share these identity commonalities. This is all a natural part of finding where we belong.

Research shows parasocial relationships can positively affect our emotions too, reducing the feelings of loneliness and offering us comfort in times of distress. This is especially true if you're more socially awkward or anxious, as parasocial relationships can support your need to feel relatedness and belonging without the vulnerability that real relationships require. But there comes a tipping point.

When parasocial relationships go beyond a healthy level of affiliation and affection, we can experience myriad negative consequences. The identity feedback loop in Chapter 1 illustrates this: when we're exposed to similar content or people constantly, we begin to over-identify with it, which undermines our self-concept and autonomy. When we over-identify with our parasocial relationships, we risk becoming enmeshed—tangling our own identity with those we admire, and unable to tell ourselves apart. When we have these extremely strong, one-sided bonds with someone, we start to wholeheartedly believe we know, and are like, this person.

Beyond the impact on our self-concept, this enmeshment leaves us vulnerable in a multitude of ways. As the conversation between me and my friends revealed, we feel real emotions—like grief, anger, betrayal and disappointment—if our parasocial relationships don't meet our expectations. As we become emotionally invested in others without reciprocity, we start to rely on them to satisfy our emotional needs. This strips our agency away, leaving us susceptible to distress when our favourite influencer makes a decision we don't agree with. What's more, this increases our unrealistic expectations of our boundaries with that person. As our emotional attachment deepens, we expect constant access to them. This is unhealthy for anyone, and it's a ridiculous expectation to hold for another human being—which is a challenge that celebrities, sportspeople and influencers alike navigate regularly.

When we're constantly comparing ourselves upwards, we also experience an erosion of self-esteem and confidence because we are idolising people and lifestyles that are out of reach. And as our attachment and perceived similarity grows, so does our susceptibility to influence and manipulation. Parasocial relationships are the perfect in-road for selling. The more we idolise someone, and the more vulnerable we feel through comparison, the more likely we are to believe what comes out of their mouth. We might start outsourcing our decisions to them—what we wear, where we holiday, how we invest, what we eat, what we believe and how we vote may all become a product of this influence. And this happens through a blend of perceived authenticity, closeness and relatability, all wrapped up in the idea of a relationship rather than a transaction.

Brands and influencers alike exploit this type of relationship to sell you things. From 'get ready with me' videos to the more direct 'buy my new face cream/coffee brand/sports apparel' social posts, your parasocial relationships arguably hold more sway over your purchase decisions than anyone else. Studies have shown that when we see influencers and celebrities as *friends*, we treat the information they share with the same validity as we would a good friend, which drastically increases our impulse to purchase.

It's estimated that the influencer economy is valued at over US$250 billion, so it's safe to say that while your favourite influencer or celebrity is probably an awesome person, they likely have an ulterior motive (money) behind their online behaviour.

Parasocial interactions can feel like a real relationship. If an influencer likes your comment or reshares your repost, we can feel we are closer to the source than we truly are. The following table outlines the key differences between parasocial relationships and the other types of relationships we form online and offline.

Friend	**Pseudo-connection**	**Parasocial relationship**
This person knows you personally (in real life and/or intimately online)	This person connects with you in-person or via social media	This person connects one-way only (the connection is not reciprocated)
This person engages in real life and on social media in a multitude of ways	This person would say hello to you and like, comment and message you about your content on social media	You have one-way interactions with this person, such as liking, commenting on and resharing their content
The relationship feels close, trusting, empathic	The relationship is surface-level, even superficial	The relationship is driven by attachment and admiration

(continued)

Friend	Pseudo-connection	Parasocial relationship
You could contact this person for support or help	You would feel uncomfortable contacting this person for support or help	You have no way to personally contact them
You share a deep connection with active engagement	You have a loose or familiar connection with active and passive engagement	You have no real connection, with passive engagement; you may be actively engaged in fandoms and associated communities

Establishing healthy boundaries around parasocial relationships

Parasocial relationships are a little like fast food—okay in moderation, but you can't sustain your diet on them alone. With the noted benefits and risks of parasocial relationships, establishing healthy boundaries around them is the best way to still enjoy the content of your favourite celebrities and influencers while maintaining a clear sense of self.

Here's a checklist to help you better understand your online relationships and moderate your reliance on parasocial relationships. Read each statement carefully and consider scoring yourself from 1–5 for each one:

1 = Not true for me, 3 = Moderately true for me, 5 = Very true for me

	Statement	Score
Awareness and understanding	I can accurately identity the different types of relationships that I have online (friends, connections, parasocial relationships)	
	I understand when an online relationship is one-sided, even if it feels emotionally real	

	Statement	Score
	I recognise that constantly viewing the intimate details of someone's life online is not the same as being part of it	
Emotional boundaries	I don't feel overly emotionally invested in the lives and decisions of the influencers and celebrities I follow	
	My mood isn't dependent on the content uploads and shares of the influencers and celebrities I follow	
	I don't feel entitled to the attention, engagement and validation of the people I follow	
Time and energy	I have clear boundaries around how much time I spend engaging in content from influencers on social media	
	My relationship with those I follow isn't replacing any real-life relationships	
	I pay attention to how my online relationships affect me, and if they're nourishing and generally positive, or they're draining	
Connection diversity	I have a good mix of different relationships online and offline, including mutual two-sided friendships	
	I participate in groups and communities that provide space for my input and ideas and offer shared connection	
Marketing awareness	I can spot content that is trying to sell me something	
	I feel in control when it comes to making decisions about what I purchase, and I don't feel compelled to purchase everything an influencer or celebrity try to sell me	
Interacting	I engage with influencers and celebrities thoughtfully, without hoping for an interaction in return	

(continued)

	Statement	Score
	I engage with friends and communities who provide an opportunity for me to feel seen, heard and connected through two-way engagement	
	I follow creators who build communities I believe in, not just followers	

Self-scoring: How many times did these statements feel true for you? Add up your total score (the maximum possible score across all 17 questions is 85):

- **0–25:** You have a high reliance on parasocial relationships and online relationships to fulfil your connection needs. There is a high chance this is impacting your real-world relationships, and your relationship to yourself.
- **25–50:** You have a moderate reliance on online relationships, and these are likely impacting your real-world relationships, decision making and relationship to yourself to a degree.
- **50–85:** You have a low reliance on online relationships, and a strong awareness of how these types of relationships impact on you, and your real-world relationships.

Wherever you find yourself on this scale, the most important first step is creating this awareness—this is where change begins.

If you find yourself in the 0–25 range, be gentle with yourself; your reliance on parasocial relationships is filling a very real need for connection, and this is an innate human need. The work, then, lies in gradually building the conditions where you can feel safe and open to pursue connection offline—with people who will reciprocate this relationship. Ultimately, this will lead to deeper feelings of connection and satisfaction in your relationships. If you're in the

25–50 range, you're sitting at a crossroads; your online relationships aren't defining you, but without intentionality you may find yourself being nudged further into reliance on them. For those scoring 50–85, you're in a strong position of self-awareness and your focus should be on continuing to nurture the relationships that feel nourishing to you.

Now that you've had an opportunity to dive deeper into your online and offline relationships, take time to reflect on what this reveals about your sense of self, and where you'd like to make changes:

1. What do my parasocial relationships reveal about my own needs, my self-concept and what my values are? Are they replacing a need that's not being met elsewhere?
2. Can I take breaks and step away from social media when I notice I am overly absorbed in someone else's life?
3. How can I create more ways to be present in my own life, and build stronger connections in real life?
4. Do my online relationships support my personal growth and future vision?

Regardless of your score out of 85, return to these reflection questions regularly as a compass to help guide your decision making.

11

The Credibility Illusion

Refreshing the postage tracking app for the tenth time that day, a jolt of excitement coursed through me as I finally read: *on board for delivery*. After trying everything, the solution to my weight loss and acne-prone skin was finally arriving, all wrapped up in pretty packaging to boot. I wondered: 'Could it really be as easy as drinking herbal tea three times a day?' Well, if the Instagram testimonials were anything to go by, then absolutely yes. Gorgeous, athleticwear-clad girls with rock-hard abs and glowing skin had been imploring me daily: 'What are you waiting for? Don't live with a bloated belly and bad skin when you don't have to!'

It was the perfect confluence of conditions: another skin breakout during a midsummer heatwave, the post-holiday I-ate-and-drank-too-much blues, and the New Year Instagram algorithm vortex. After two weeks of consistent content showing me beautiful, glowing and impossibly fit women who were encouraging me to join them every time I opened my phone, I caved—succumbing to the ease of the swipe-up. Ordering my first month's supply of an Insta-famous detox tea, I felt excited and hopeful. Was this the time I'd finally get in shape and start feeling good about myself?

The red flags arrived early but, convinced by the overwhelming social proof, I stuck with it. Three times a day, one scoop of the herbal blend: morning, noon and evening. That was it. Simple. If I could keep it up to the end of the month it would all be worth it. My skin would be glowing. My stomach would be flat. Except, that's not at all what happened.

By day three, I couldn't sleep. Wired, I tossed and turned all night, exhausted but buzzing. By day five, I reached a new low. My lack of sleep was compounded by the near-constant urge to go to the toilet. It seemed my digestive system was cleansing itself of absolutely everything, every hour. After just seven days I was down two kilograms. Sure, I was feeling lighter, but I was a puffy-eyed, energyless zombie. The promised glow hadn't arrived.

And yet, I persevered. Surely this would get easier, right? Wrong. By the end of week two, I was on the brink of a meltdown—I was sleeping poorly, irritable and sallow—but another two kilograms down. I'd lost more weight in a fortnight than I had from years of cardio and dieting. But behind the weight loss was a brutal irony: in an attempt to make my body look better, I'd made myself feel far worse on the inside.

Calling it quits mid-detox made me feel like a failure. How was it so hard to drink tea for a month? Why was it so impossible for me to just stick to the plan? Dejected, I shared my woes with a girlfriend who was also a nutritionist. She offered to take a look at the tea.

'You've been drinking this three times a day? And before bed?' she exclaimed. 'No wonder you can't sleep and keep running to the bathroom!'

Confused, I responded 'Why, what's in it? The advertisement said it was just natural metabolic support.'

'It's natural, sure, it contains guarana, and that's four times the recommended daily intake of caffeine, for goodness' sake,' she said. 'How this doesn't come with a warning label is beyond me!'

Feeling stupid, I threw the rest of the tea out. How had I managed to be so thoroughly duped without properly looking into it? I am university-educated, trained in psychological sciences, with a decade of experience in marketing, and I had still been convinced, in a moment of vulnerability, to buy a completely unproven diet supplement no qualified health professional had recommended. All it took was a few fit girls and a handful of well-curated Instagram reels. I felt like a bona-fide idiot.

But I know I'm not alone here. Social media is a masterclass of illusion. With the right mix of clever messaging, emotional resonance and visual appeal, delivered at a moment of vulnerability, it can make almost anything seem credible. The hook wasn't just the promise of transformation. It was the carefully embedded credibility cues that sold the illusion: practiced vulnerability, repetition and social proof from aspirational bodies showing me just how life-changing the tea had supposedly been. This carefully curated blend of cues had convinced me it was the silver bullet to my woes.

I wish I was able to say my skinny-tea saga was the first and only time I was duped online, but it wasn't. From snail-secretion facemasks to grass-flavoured smoothie powders, well-crafted Instagram reels have sold me more pseudo-solutions to my modern-day problems than I care to admit. So how does social media create the illusion of credibility so successfully?

It's tempting to believe that before social media, it was easy to discern fact from fiction—but this simply isn't the case. Even trusted institutional and media outlets have long histories of curating information through the lenses of power, politics and persuasion. Governments use propaganda, companies fund research, news media companies publish what businesses pay for—these are not conspiracies. Previously, trust was built on access, authority and familiarity, to the exclusion of many voices. Fast-forward to the digital era and what's changed isn't the presence of manipulation in what we read and hear, but the speed in which it hits us and saturates our perception.

Now everyone has access to the game.

Misinformation, disinformation, fake news and conspiracy theories have always existed. But who creates and shares this information has now shifted—it's been democratised in its production and amplified in its reach by algorithms, without any checking mechanisms. Information propagation has shifted from traditional gatekeepers and into the hands of each and every one of us, which is a profound, and sometimes worrying, shift.

While the shift in information propagation appears to be a net positive—it's been crucial for social movements, for minority groups and in times of disaster, to name a few—the onslaught of information at our fingertips is overwhelming. Evolutionarily our brains are wired for efficiency, not careful discernment, leaving us more confused, exhausted and susceptible than ever as we attempt to wade through myriad competing truths that are vying for our attention and engagement... and money.

We're living through a *credibility crisis*—one that didn't start with social media but is now impossible to ignore. Misinformation and fake news is rife, and yet somewhere among it all lies verifiable, trustworthy and competent sources. We just need to know how to find them.

Let's explore what credibility looks like in the age of social media, and how your thoughts, feelings and relationships with other online users (and influencers) impact how you view information. With this understanding, you can then recalibrate how to decide what information to believe and vet the sources for yourself—and avoid any unnecessary tea detoxes in the process!

Why we trust the wrong opinions

The online world is brimming with information updated at a pace so rapid our human brain simply cannot keep up—and we shouldn't try to. Instead of being swept up in velocity and overwhelmed by online news, it's a superpower to be able to create the space to slow down, dig deeper and find truly credible information for yourself. But as our lives feel busier than ever, we often outsource our thinking to others—rather than taking the time to validate information, we simply absorb what's put in front of us by algorithms in 30-second snippets from influencers we like. As a result, the proliferation of fake news, misinformation, disinformation and conspiracy theories has never been more apparent, and it has become harder than ever to tell these apart from credible sources.

According to sociologist Robert Gass, source credibility is one of the most robust forms of social influence. Source credibility is defined as the extent to which we perceive someone to be trustworthy and expert, which influences our willingness to accept and believe their message. For example, researchers Nicolas Guéguen and Nathalie Pichot found pedestrians were more likely to ignore a 'no crossing' light and jaywalk when following a well-dressed person than a poorly dressed person, signalling that appearances influence our perception of credibility. In the world of social media, a multitude of cues can proxy for expertise and trustworthiness, and these can make us susceptible to believing the *wrong* people: people who look credible, but aren't.

Social media is a breeding ground for *surface credibility*: trust built on aesthetic appeal, vanity metrics and concise (yet often reductive) information presented with confidence and conviction. These credibility cues mimic expertise, and as a result we mistake them for trustworthiness. Surface credibility appeals because it looks good, talks slick, feels relatable and removes the need for us to dig any deeper. In a busy world, it seemingly simplifies the complex, often incorrectly. This type of credibility is a fallacy, and it seldom replaces the substantive source credibility we should be relying on to validate factual information.

Our feelings of connection and attachment towards those we follow play a part in how we perceive their credibility, too. Who we feel an affiliation with or affection towards online influences our thoughts and behaviour, sometimes even more so than those with expertise in the field. When presented with content from people we admire, like sportspeople or celebrities, we're more susceptible to surface cues of credibility—engagement metrics, aesthetic content, relatability, confidence and conviction—which is why we end up judging an influencer's advice on a diet trend over that of a qualified nutritionist, even when we *probably* know better.

Our brains crave stability, certainty and simplicity: when we're presented with simple answers to challenging questions by people we trust, and people we identify with, it satisfies our short-term cognitive needs. We no longer have to waste our precious cognitive energy thinking, worrying or deliberating—we can just act on what we're being told. Easy. The trouble is, we're making ill-informed decisions based on opinions that lack verifiable expertise and evidence, which forgoes meeting our longer-term needs: an actual solution.

This matters because every time we choose surface credibility over substantive credibility, we're allowing ourselves to be misinformed, which doesn't just impact the decision at hand but how we seek and relate to information generally. The more we outsource our decision making to those with surface credibility, the more we're training our judgement to be based on surface cues over verifiable expertise, quick solutions over evidence. This erodes our ability to discern fact from fiction, and we slowly lose touch with what trustworthy information looks and sounds like.

Surface credibility versus substantive credibility

Here's a cheat sheet for separating surface from substantive credibility, so you can spot this for yourself.

Surface credibility	Substantive credibility
Likes, followers and engagement	Formal qualifications, experience and expertise
Overly simplified or reductive explanations for complex scenarios	Acknowledgement of nuance, complexity and limitations of current research and knowledge
Relies heavily on anecdote and novelty	Rigorous research supplemented with case examples
Certainty, conviction, confidence	Cautious, curious, conservative
Blue ticks and verification badges administered by social platforms	Peer reviewed research, published work, citations, academic community trust
Viral and trending content	Meaningful and robust contributions to public discourse
Opinion/expertise spread laterally across a number of topics (run outside their lane)	Deep and concise expertise on one or few limited areas (run inside their lane, and admit knowledge gaps elsewhere)
Product/brand placement or affiliation	No ulterior motive, or sales benefit

A substantive credibility source *can* also have a number or all of the surface credibility cues, too, but a truly credible source can't *only* have surface-level cues. This creates the illusion of credibility without substantive depth, and the information the source provides should be treated as opinion rather than expertise, accordingly.

Surface credibility cues attract attention, but alone they are not signals of trustworthiness, expertise or credibility. Substantive credibility is generally more 'boring' because it's less clickable and doesn't offer silver-bullet solutions; it's slower to build hype around, but it's far more reliable. As the old adage reminds us: if it looks too good to be true, it probably is.

How your cognitive biases double-down on surface credibility

Our brains are incredibly efficient at processing information, but because of this they often lead us astray. Your brain is faced with millions of data points to process every day: everything you see, hear, smell, touch, taste and feel has to be processed, filtered and prioritised by your brain so that you can make sense of the world. Most of this happens unconsciously, and to process all of this your brain creates mental shortcuts (called *heuristics*) that simplify this complex information.

Without these mental shortcuts the world would be overwhelming, but with any shortcut there come trade-offs. Heuristics rely on our past experiences, emotions and gut instincts to make judgements, rather than slowly deliberated rational thought. It means even when we think we're being logical, we're often relying on automatic processing using heuristics or cognitive biases to make fast decisions.

The late psychologist Daniel Kahneman calls this *System 1* thinking: fast, automatic and intuitive, this system is always on, and we rely on it with minimal effort. But when it comes to processing information on social media, it's really *System 2* thinking we need: slow, deliberate and analytical. Kahneman's book *Thinking, Fast and Slow* urges us to challenge our initial System 1 thinking to go beyond the easy and automatic processing. This is so we can slow down, weigh evidence and dive beyond surface credibility to look deeper. Some decisions can be safely made with System 1 thinking—like routine, low stakes choices—but some decisions, like those linked to our health, wealth and relationships, call for us to slow down and deliberate. This helps us to make more informed, expertly guided judgement calls.

The following table provides a quick breakdown of System 1 and System 2 thinking.

System 1 thinking	**System 2 thinking**
Fast, automatic, effortless	Slow, deliberate, effortful
Relies on mental shortcuts (heuristics), biases and intuition	Uses logic, evidence and information processing
Operates instantly—in milliseconds	Operates slowly—in seconds and minutes
Offers certainty and conviction	Often feels uncertain, even contradictory
Susceptible to manipulation, bias and surface credibility	Better at spotting errors, interrogating sources and weighing nuance
Best for low stakes, routine and familiar decisions	Best for high stakes, complex and unfamiliar decisions
Example: Judging someone's mood based on their tone; preferring one photograph over another at a quick glance.	Example: Making decisions about your health; deciding where to invest your money.

System 1 and System 2 thinking are both forms of information processing in our brain, and one isn't inherently better than the other. What's important is to know when we're using System 1 thinking when we should be slowing down and engaging System 2. Social media thrives on System 1 thinking; with its quick reactions, fast reels and snappy soundbites, it amplifies the volume and velocity of the information we need to process. And because of this, we get stuck in autopilot: processing without consideration and making snap judgements without verification—the very environment surface credibility thrives in. But when you slow down, dive deeper and get curious before making a decision, you can begin to tap into System 2 thinking and find your way to accessing substance credibility.

Making sense of heuristics

In a pre-digital era, when we weren't processing the volume of information we now are, heuristics worked more effectively. Here are some examples of the heuristics your brain relies on to process information.

Heuristic	Source	Outcome
Authority	We trusted qualified sources like doctors, professors and journalists.	'This person is a qualified source. I should rely on their opinion.'
Reputation	We trusted word of mouth, testimonials and expert consensus.	'If others trust this person, I probably can, too.'
Knowledge/ expertise	We trusted scarcity signals like degrees, books and peer-reviewed publications.	'The information source is verified, therefore it can be trusted.'
Feedback	We would cross-reference decisions within expert communities.	'If multiple sources lead to the same suggestion, it's probably the right decision.'
Familiarity	We trusted people/ situations known to us.	'I've seen this before, so it's likely true.'

This isn't to say that these mental shortcuts didn't create errors in judgement—they weren't a perfect system. However, because the velocity and the volume of information was slower, the signals of credibility were relatively stable and harder to manipulate.

In the short period of time (relative to human evolution) that social media and the internet have existed, the way information has been presented to us has drastically shifted. The problem is that our brains haven't kept up. How we process information, using heuristics and biases as shortcuts, has remained the same. As a result, these mental shortcuts—which rely on reliable input cues—are being hijacked and exploited, replaced with surface credibility that our brain mistakenly conflates with substance.

And when the brain gets it wrong, this can lead to errors in thinking. But it's not your fault; your brain is using its mental shortcuts to conserve energy, but it's distorting your view of credibility.

As well as my skinny tea diet mishap, here's another (hypothetical) example to explain how such errors in thinking arise via social media. Imagine you're scrolling on Instagram and you land on an influencer who's confidently explaining how an all-meat diet is the answer to all your health challenges. They're super-fit and attractive, their video is slick and professional looking, they're using bold captions and they are speaking with utter conviction.

You think, 'Wow, they look incredible so they're obviously on to something.'

Except they're not a doctor. They're not a dietitian, or a nutritionist. They're a fitness influencer being paid by a meat subscription brand that cites one article on meat consumption and claims the associated health benefits based on a study on rats. But they may still win you over because:

1. **They speak confidently:** Therefore, you assumed authority (heuristic)
2. **They are attractive and well lit:** Therefore, you succumbed to the halo effect (cognitive bias)

3. **The product keeps showing up in your feed:** Therefore, the repetition increases your familiarity (heuristic)
4. **The product is being shared by other fitness influencers:** Thus creating a bandwagon effect (cognitive bias)

You start to believe them. It's the perfect storm of surface credibility cues meeting mental shortcuts to create errors in your judgement that arise from your cognitive biases. Maybe you even stop eating vegetables—such is the power of misinformation when it accumulates. You wholeheartedly believe this is the right call.

Heuristics and cognitive biases don't just shape what we believe, but also our *conviction* in those beliefs. They drive overconfidence, even in the face of contrary evidence and logic. This is a clear call to action to slow down, deliberate and move into System 2 thinking before making a decision.

Common cognitive biases

Here are some of the most common cognitive biases you're likely to be unconsciously using to process information on social media.

Bias	**Effect**	**Outcome**
Confirmation bias	We seek information that confirms what we already think, believe and feel.	We reinforce existing beliefs and negate or ignore contrary evidence, opinions or viewpoints.
Familiarity heuristic	We begin to believe things are true because we see them so often.	Repeated exposure, even to false claims, makes them feel credible over time.
Halo effect	We see one positive trait in someone (such as their appearance) as indicative of their whole.	We're more likely to see someone as being trustworthy, credible or an expert because they're attractive or confident.

Bias	Effect	Outcome
Bandwagon effect	We adopt beliefs, behaviours or viewpoints because others are doing it.	We believe something to be true or credible because it's gone viral or others are doing it.
Authority bias	We trust perceived figures of authority, regardless of actual expertise.	We place higher value on the opinions of unqualified influencers, celebrities and even politicians over those with substantive credibility in the field.
Dunning-Kruger effect	People with lower expertise tend to overestimate their actual knowledge.	Overconfident takes from influencers with no actual qualification in the subject area are amplified by their audience.
In-group bias	We tend to favour information from people we feel are relatable or we identify with.	We believe information from our tribes and echo chambers without question, dismissing outsiders.
Affect heuristic	We rely on emotional rather than logical evaluation.	We take information that 'feels right' to be true over what is factually correct.
Negativity bias	We pay more attention to negative rather than positive information.	We fixate on things that create outrage and fear rather than facts and balanced information.
Cognitive dissonance	We seek to avoid information that disconfirms our beliefs and opinions.	To avoid discomfort, we attack, unfollow or troll opinions, information or people that challenge our worldview.

The same innate cognitive processes—like heuristics and biases—that once helped us quickly make sense of the complex world around us are now fuelled by misinformation, polarisation and echo chambers. What's more, research has found that facts alone often don't change our minds, especially when what we believe is connected to our identity. For example, if we're in an echo chamber that confirms our beliefs around certain information, we tend to double-down, even if contradictory information is presented to us.

What's interesting is that we're actually more aware than ever of how much misinformation exists—we just don't know how to filter it. Rationally, we know that social media is rife with manipulative tactics designed to make us think, feel and act in certain ways, and yet we still succumb to its effects. And our frustration at this becomes misdirected. As we become more unsure of who and what to trust, we double-down inside our tribes and echo chambers, and we discredit validated sources. The more this occurs, the more the algorithm takes over—reinforcing the beliefs we tightly hold by showing us more of them in our feed, which diminishes our cognitive autonomy and our access to contrary worldviews. This gives us a false sense of confidence: we feel informed while being systematically misinformed within the algorithmic echo chamber.

This is a dangerous cocktail, as what we think we know to be true—which includes our own opinions, heuristics and cognitive biases—is mirrored back to us by the algorithms as they falsely confirm these beliefs.

There's a rule of thumb we use in science that can be applied here: a good scientist always seeks to *disprove* their hypothesis. In other words, if you believe something to be vehemently true, find and interrogate all of the information that disproves it… if you come to the same conclusions, then you'll *really* know if it's true.

Figure 11.1 shows how we can remain stuck in shallow loops of information exposure when we allow our cognitive biases and heuristics to go unchecked when using social media. When we interrogate what we're seeing with more thoughtfulness and rigour, we create the space for deeper, more complex thought and information exposure. This calls for us to search more widely for information sources, rather than relying solely on surface credibility and algorithmically recommended content.

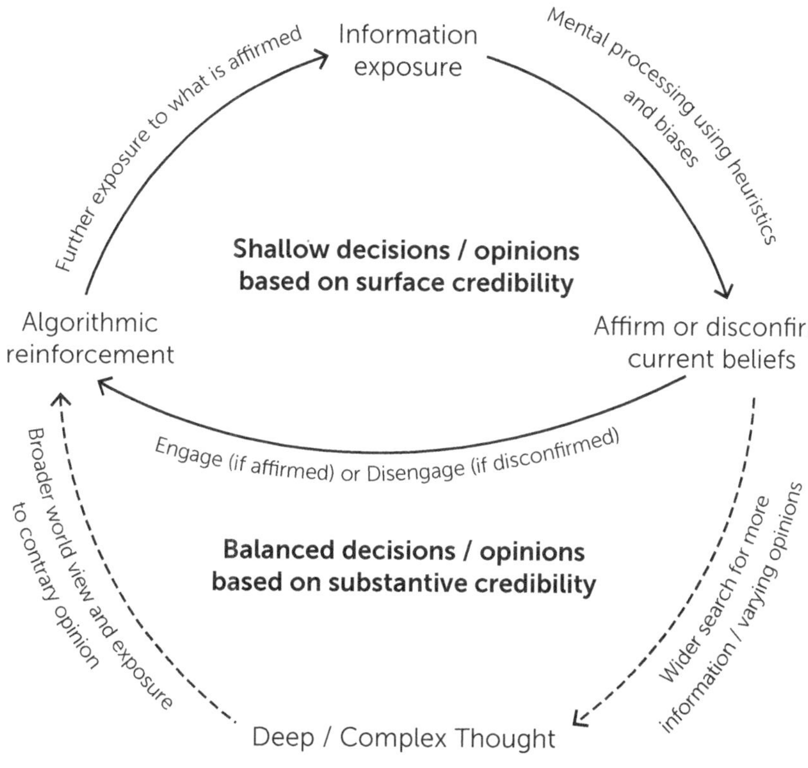

Figure 11.1 How unchecked mental processing leads to reliance on surface credibility cues and algorithmic reinforcement.

Why it's hard to leave

We've all felt it before—the irresistible pull to stay in an online space, even when you know it's not good for you. Maybe it's a creator you know you should unfollow, a group chat that's turned toxic, an online community that you've outgrown or a social media platform that isn't adding value to your life. You want to leave, but you just don't feel like you can.

This is because your brain—and your identity—is doing its best to keep you there. When we encounter influencers and online communities that validate our beliefs, we get a dopamine hit that chemically reinforces our desire to stay (similar to the habit loops discussed in Chapter 5). The algorithm perpetuates this by serving up more content you're likely to agree with, which reinforces your feelings of validation in those spaces.

And as we've just uncovered, when we encounter information that confirms our beliefs, opinions and worldview, we're more likely to engage with it. Our heuristics and cognitive biases, such as the confirmation bias, unconsciously cause us to seek out information that reinforces our views. Our identity is entangled in this process—the more we engage, the more we enmesh our ideologies and online affiliations with our self-concept. This identity-fusion occurs when our sense of self starts to merge with the opinions, groups and affiliations we hold online. So, leaving an online space isn't just about deleting an app. It can feel like a fundamental betrayal not just of the group, but of yourself.

When our identity feels deeply connected to what we believe and our online affiliations, contradictory evidence and viewpoints feel like a threat. More autonomous thinking comes when we intentionally invite divergent perspectives and opinions into our world. This is a radical reclamation of our personal agency.

Reclaiming your digital decision making

Social media distorts what you see as credible, so what are the checks and balances for better digital decision making?

First, let's look at how a decision should be made. Start by asking yourself:

- Am I reacting quickly because it seems easy, obvious or certain? *(If the answer is yes, it means you're likely in System 1 thinking. The next question will help you decide if you should slow down.)*
- Is this decision high stakes and/or unfamiliar to me? *(If the decision is high stakes or unfamiliar, this is an indication that System 2 thinking might be needed—take time to slow down, and deliberate further.)*
- Do I have enough reliable, verifiable and expert information to make an informed decision? *(If the answer is no, where could you find more information, outside of social media, that will help you make an informed decision?)*
- If I had to explain my reasoning to someone else, could I do that with actual evidence or just gut instinct? *(If the answer is gut instinct alone, you should consider if more information is needed to make a truly informed decision.)*
- Would the decision look different if I took 10 minutes, or one hour, or a week to decide? *(System 1 thinking feels urgent; to tap in to System 2 thinking, take time to slow down and deliberate—this might reveal a different answer than your initial reaction.)*

(continued)

Now, interrogate your information sources so you can discern between surface and substantive credibility:

- What qualifications does this person hold to speak on this subject matter?
- Am I influenced by their confidence or actual expertise?
- What evidence do they give to support this claim? Is it substantive (peer-reviewed, evidence)?
- Would I still believe this if it wasn't trending?
- Are they actually a reliable source, or just relatable?

Now, check if there are any cognitive biases at play:

- Am I only following them because they agree with me (my beliefs, opinions)?
- Am I automatically trusting what's familiar and comforting?
- When was the last time I changed my mind, or felt like I wanted to?
- Do I follow anyone who I disagree with or whose opinions feel threatening?

Biases are not a weakness; they're simply a feature of your brain. But to keep them in check, we need to actively push ourselves outside our comfort zone to seek opinions that might disprove our own beliefs and opinions.

Finally, take a step outside the tribe and echo chamber and ask yourself:

- Can I hold the ideas of others with curiosity rather than judgement?
- Am I open and curious, or more concerned with being right?

- Can I allow my worldview to evolve with new information, rather than stay the same?
- Can I comfortably be around people who challenge me, rather than only people who agree with me?

Credibility extends beyond who you trust—it fundamentally shifts how you experience the world and, when you're open to it, expands your ability to question yourself.

PART IV

Living REAL: Reconnecting to Yourself

This section is where you apply what we've covered to chart a new course forward for yourself.

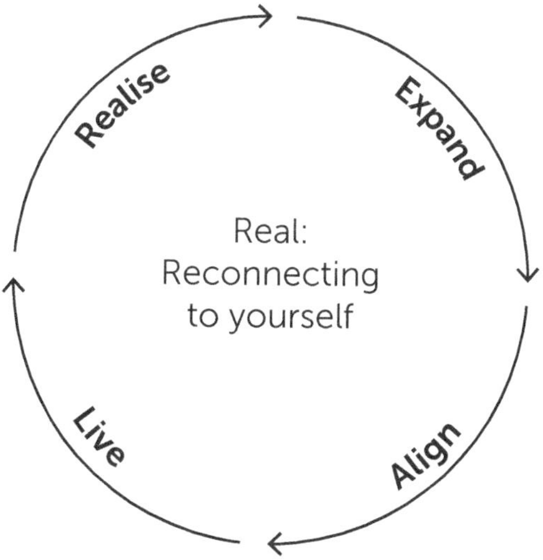

You'll move from *realising* the systems social media ensnares us in to *expanding* beyond this and diving deeper into understanding yourself. You'll build new structures that *align* behaviour with intention, before stepping into *living* a life that belongs to you.

You'll reconnect to what truly matters to you and redefine living meaningfully—beyond social media validation—to establish practices and new habits that help you live this every day.

Before we dive in, let's get clear on one thing: I'm not going to tell you to quit social media. It's a part of modern life and has the potential to be truly valuable. Instead, we'll explore how to recalibrate your relationship with it, so it aligns with the life you're intentionally building.

12

REALISE—A System of Relevance, Not Meaning

We live in a time when it's never been easier to be visible, but it's immensely harder to feel understood. We can post a photo, a reel or a comment that's viewed by thousands and still feel *unseen*. We're constantly connected to everyone, yet we feel deeply disconnected from ourselves. This is the contradiction of social media: while it gives us a feeling of relevance through validation and affirmation, it can't offer us a meaningful life.

Realising this is the system that we exist inside underlies everything. We can't change what we can't name.

Instead of connection, we're constantly comparing. And instead of feeling contentment, we're content optimising—replacing purpose with pings, and critical thinking with algorithmic recommendations. Social media has taught us that if we're being noticed, we hold value. It encourages us to measure our worth via engagement and followers. And as we perform for relevance, we unknowingly move further away from what matters: further away from ourselves.

Social media keeps us stuck on the surface. And what we find on the surface is rarely what contributes to a *meaningful* life.

Meaning can only be found when we dive deeper. Beyond image and social approval, meaning asks us to consider what gives our life substance, *purpose*—a reason to wake up every day. It can't be found in the instant gratification of curating content; it's a slow-burn revelation that comes from our connection to self. And we can't find that depth when we're treading water on the surface.

Many of us have spent too long stuck on the surface—myself included. Not because we lack depth, but because we've forgotten there's more to us than the fragments we share on social media. *We are more than our profile self.*

Social media is purposely designed to keep us stuck on the surface, preoccupied by surface-level concerns. It distracts us from the deeper questions by telling us we're relevant in the moment. Likes, comments and shares keep us hooked in the pursuit of instant pleasure and validation. We avoid discomfort, numb boredom and scroll through stress, looking for cheap thrills, while our deeper needs go unmet. And the satisfaction is always short-lived, because it's just an illusion of comfort. What we really need is purpose, connection and a sense of contribution—needs these apps were never designed to fulfil—and yet we keep scrolling, searching.

By design, social media keeps us perpetually chasing relevance, but what we really need is *meaning*. And it's through meaning that we come to reconnect with our *real* selves.

Beyond feeling good to living well

Social media feels compelling because it taps into our natural human need to feel good. We seek pleasure, comfort and novelty, and it delivers these with little effort. Instant likes, shares and comments give us fleeting boosts of validation and approval, while scrolling offers a way to procrastinate, helping us avoid discomfort and providing a needed distraction when we're stressed.

Psychologists call this *hedonic wellbeing*: our innate tendency to seek pleasure and avoid discomfort. And there's nothing inherently wrong with seeking pleasure—joy, comfort and ease are all important parts of being human. The problem is, we've come to conflate feeling good with living a good life. And the two are not the same.

And as social media allows us to over-indulge in these quick-win, pleasurable, avoidance behaviours, we forgo a more fulfilling form of nourishment: nourishment that comes from *eudaimonic wellbeing*, which is a deeper sense of wellbeing derived from meaningfulness, belonging, personal growth and contribution. These are things not easily found in the tiny squares of an Instagram grid, even though that's where we often expect to find them. While scrolling might alleviate boredom, and a few direct messages mimic closeness, these are fleeting reassurances and don't satiate our thirst for a life rich with purpose and connection. In short: social media offers easy pleasure, but it doesn't give you deeper fulfilment.

Meaning, connection and contribution are needs we all seek, but we're often misguided about how to find them. To move away from the surface, we need to be brave and willing to explore what truly matters to us.

The fragility of relevance

When our sense of self is contingent on relevance, we become fragile. Our ego relies on being buoyed by external validation—a fickle and uncontrollable variable. One day we're getting attention; the next, crickets. We're always riding the wave of likes, comments and the algorithm's whims, which are unstable and fleeting. And as you start relying on relevance as a metric of self-worth, it becomes utterly consuming as you feel compelled to feed the monster to stay relevant. It's in this way that *you become more of what you perform* on social media.

This is why chasing relevance on social media feels exhausting—it's an ever-moving target that only buys cheap relief. You're stuck in an endless loop of impression management. But meaning works much differently.

To live a more meaningful life, we need to reprioritise our time and energy away from instant gratification and short-term wins. Instead, we need to expect a slow burn. We have to be willing to engage in our own lives in a deeper way: commit to things that challenge us, invest in friendships and relationships for the long haul, and contribute to our community and the world around us in a way that adds value to the lives of others. And we need to be willing to deprioritise social media *approval* to do this.

Researchers Michael Steger, Todd Kashdan and Shigehiro Oishi found that when we pursue purpose, meaning and connection we actually *feel* better about ourselves and are more satisfied with our lives. They call it 'feeling good by doing good'. Meaning doesn't always feel exciting in the moment, and we don't always have something to instantly show for it, but it's through creating a meaningful life that we find a sense of happiness and contentment. We find *depth.*

Here's a simple equation to make sense of this:

> **Meaning + Purpose + Growth** = *Deeper satisfaction and wellbeing over time*

Alternatively, this is how the equation looks when we prioritise relevance:

> **Pleasure + Comfort + Pain avoidance** = *Temporary relief, with short-term benefits*

What's more, when we prioritise relevance over meaning repeatedly—like we do when we're using social media—we're prone to what psychologists call *hedonic adaptation*: we get used to the instant pleasure and relief it gives us, and crave more and more as a result. So, while social media hooks you on chasing relevance, it feels less and less satisfying over time. The result? You become so preoccupied with living a life through your screen, you forget what actually makes life worth living.

Realising your unmet needs

There's nothing inherently wrong with a desire to feel relevant. It's innately human to want to be seen, to be acknowledged and to matter. But the system of social media confuses being noticed for being *known*—and visibility doesn't meet our needs in the same way as being valued and feeling connected does.

Often, when we reach for our phone, we're trying to fulfil a need. Before we progress to reframing our behaviours on social media, it's helpful to first just witness our relationship with it. This is where we begin to realise how we've been trying to use social media to meet some of our unmet needs.

Over the next few days, pay attention to the moments when:

- You reach for your phone without thinking
- You feel the urge to check if things are being seen, commented on or liked
- You compare your life to someone you're seeing on social media
- You feel a hit of validation from social media, or the absence of such validation

(continued)

And without judgement, gently ask yourself: 'What am I really seeking at this moment?'

Beneath the surface, you'll likely find it's something deeper than relevance. But, for now, just notice, as the very act of noticing is creating space for change.

Once you *realise* the pull of relevance, and how social media amplifies this need, you can't unsee it.

13

EXPAND—What You Actually Need to Thrive

What does it look like to thrive without the total absence of social media? It requires us to *expand* beyond relevance and social validation, so we can reconnect with experiences, challenges and relationships that fulfil our deeper psychological needs.

Social media, although globally accessible, actually shrinks our frame of reference over time. As we perform our profile self, engage in content loops and measure our worth against these metrics, what we view to be important compresses. Expansion happens when we move beyond this. It occurs when we welcome real, uncertain and embodied experiences back into our lives. These provide a richness to the quality of our lives.

Psychologists Richard Ryan and Edward Deci found everyone has three core psychological needs crucial to thriving—this is called *self-determination theory*, which was introduced in Chapter 7. When we actively pursue these needs, we experience deeper meaning and better wellbeing as a result. These needs offer us a framework we can use to expand beyond the confines of social media metrics so we can understand our core needs more deeply, as well as provide direction for action.

The three psychological needs are autonomy, competency and relatedness:

- We need **autonomy:** the sense that our life is our own, we have the freedom to choose and we feel we are in control of our lives.
- We need to feel **competent:** capable of learning, growing, mastering new skills and handling all that life throws at us.
- We need to feel **relatedness:** a sense of connectedness to others—a feeling that we belong and we're part of a community.

In short, you need to feel in control of your life, you need to feel like you're good at stuff, and you need to feel connected to other people. If you're missing these needs right now, there's a good chance you won't feel like you're thriving. When these needs are chronically neglected, you're going to feel unfulfilled, adrift and insecure.

This is often where social media trips us up. It creates an illusion of autonomy by giving us seemingly endless choices, yet it's controlling our options through algorithmic suggestions that filter what we see. Every recommended post and curated advertisement pushes us further towards a narrower, more filtered version of who we are.

It induces our *feelings* of competence; as we view and absorb others performing tasks masterfully, we mistakenly think we'll increase our competence via osmosis. But this is not the case. Competence is only achieved through effort. And this effort requires commitment and friction: learning, trying, failing and trying again, until—eventually—you master the skill. There's no shortcut to mastery.

It also mimics relatedness through those always-there pseudo-connections that don't really meet our deeper needs for closeness and bonding.

Social media offers the appearance of expansion while never delivering on the real thing. To meet our psychological needs, we need to go beyond.

Meaning asks more, and gives more

We've been sold a lie: that the goal in life is to feel good all the time; that feeling constant positivity and good vibes are the only way to live. This is both wildly unrealistic and untrue. Life is full of challenges, discomfort and dark emotions, but what makes life rich is our capacity to experience it all. A meaningful life comes from aligning with what matters, not what feels or looks good.

When we're thriving, we experience both a deep sense of meaningfulness and satisfaction with our lives. But this doesn't happen by accident. It's the result of intentional decisions and actions that align with our deeper sense of self. It's not reliant on how things look on the surface, or if others approve of our choices—it's reliant on *how you feel* about the life you're living.

What's more, research by Todd Kashdan and Jonathan Rottenberg shows that when we prioritise meaningfulness over short-term gratification, we become more psychologically flexible. This is because when we're connected to what matters, we find more grit and we become better able to roll with the punches to achieve our goals. Conversely, when we're focused on the surface—chasing only fleeting feel-good emotions—we're more susceptible to the volatility of life's ups and downs. This is why when we chase happiness and contentment through quick wins, we're likely to come up short. Instead, when we pursue what feels meaningful to us, what challenges us and what keeps us engaged, we're likely to experience happiness and contentment as a result.

So, what gives your life a sense of meaning? If you're anything like me, after a lifetime of social media use, that question feels hard to answer. It could look like a creative or physical endeavour that requires your focus and sustained commitment. It might be learning a new skill like playing an instrument, learning to dance or sewing your own clothes—pursuits where betterment requires commitment and a willingness to be bad at something before you become good at it. Meaningfulness also comes from our relationships, perhaps through supporting a friend during a tough time or stepping up in your community to contribute where it's needed. In all instances, the emotional payoff is rarely instant; in fact, sometimes we'll feel uncomfortable, frustrated or unsure for a while. But over time these meaningful activities create something intrinsic that no volume of likes can replace: a sense that you're in control of your life, pursuing things of purpose and feeling connected to others. It belongs to you—this is what feels *expansive*.

Meaning is so critical to wellbeing: it offers a much studier, more robust foundation than relevance ever can. Relevance fixates on attention; meaning provides direction.

Note: It's also vital to acknowledge the factors outside our individual control that impact on our experience of life, from the cost of living to global wars and geopolitical crises, everyday racism and systemic inequity, gendered violence and access to healthcare. All these factors, and many more, play a contributing role in how you experience the world around you, which is why wellbeing should never be framed as a purely individual responsibility. While it's crucial you take accountability for yourself and focus on making change within your reach, we cannot simply 'self-care' ourselves beyond these structural realities. We can, however, choose how we respond to, participate in and play a role in influencing the world around us.

The courage to dive deeper

Choosing meaning over validation doesn't mean you need to ditch social media altogether, but it means refusing to let it dictate what you value and your worth. When you recalibrate your choices towards meaning, you stop outsourcing your autonomy and worth to algorithms and instant gratification. You rely less on the validation of others, and more on your internal compass.

Many of us have become fluent in the language of social media performance but bereft in the language of our own needs. Diving deeper requires courage, because it asks you to peel back the layers of influence and spend time reconnecting to yourself. It's a return to yourself, to your own voice and to meeting your own needs.

Diving deeper doesn't guarantee feeling good all the time, and it *shouldn't*. We mistakenly assume that our life is only going well when things are feeling positive. A life of meaning, one that's truly expansive, welcomes the good times along with the challenges—accepting both as necessary.

Emotions, like happiness, are a byproduct of a life well-lived, not a goal to be pursued outright. And thriving is an *outcome*: something you experience as a result of your decisions. It's not something you do.

A pathway to expansion

After spending years under the influence of social media, I'd lost track of what really lit me up and gave me a sense of meaning. I felt lost, adrift and without a map back to myself. What was I good at? What brought me joy? Did I really have true friends, or just social media ones? I realised answering these questions was the map back to myself that I was missing.

(continued)

Have you felt like this, too? If so, I assure you, clarity is possible. And with it comes the opportunity to chart a new course: a pathway of expansion deep with meaning over relevance.

On a piece of paper or in a notepad, take time to reflect on the following prompts and *write* (not type) your answers.

Expanding through autonomy:

1. What would I do more of if I wasn't afraid of being judged by others?
2. What values do I want to live by, even when no-one else is watching?
3. What is something I would like to do differently, even if it challenges others' assumptions of me?

Expanding through competency:

1. When was the last time I learned something new that challenged me?
2. When was the last time I tried something I was truly bad at?
3. When was the last time I felt I had mastered something difficult?

Expanding through relatedness:

1. When was the last time I had a deep, connected conversation with a friend?
2. What is something I enjoy doing in the presence of others?
3. What is something I would like others to truly know and understand about me?

Casting away:

1. What do I keep doing for the approval of others, even though it doesn't feel true for me?
2. What gives me a sense of validation, even though it doesn't feel fulfilling?

Charting a course to expansion

Now you have a better understanding of what expansion feels like for you, it's time to create a course of action you can follow to begin doing this. Draw a line down the middle of a fresh page, and in column A write 'What makes me feel relevant?' and in column B write 'What gives me a sense of meaning?'

Here's what this looks like for me.

What makes me feel relevant? *(surface)*	**What gives me a sense of meaning? *(deep)***
Posting a photo that gets a lot of likes and comments	Presenting a challenging project at work that the team took months to complete
When a lot of people like or agree with a comment I made on a post	Having a good conversation with a friend over coffee that shares my love of books
When someone new or cool follows my account	Doing something fun with my family, like going on a bike ride or camping for the weekend
When someone I admire likes or replies to a comment I made	Learning a new skill like gardening so I can grow my own fruit and vegetables at home
Getting a DM from someone about something I posted	Contributing to my local community by volunteering at the local surfing club
Finding a new account with tonnes of followers who shares my opinions and viewpoints	Taking time out for myself to slow down, meditate and do some writing

(continued)

Now, reflecting on *your* column B, take time to answer the following:

1. When was the last time I prioritised these? (Or the last time you did any of them?)
2. How could you make a small shift of time and energy to prioritise these this week?

The journey of finding more meaningfulness and expansion doesn't need to be a dramatic deep dive. Often, it's more of a quiet and intentional return to what truly matters to you. As you'll see from your list, meaning isn't something you find on a screen—it's something you experience by connecting to what lights you up from the inside. It's what happens when you stop performing and start living.

The truth is that in our modern world, staying attuned to what's meaningful to you is tough—it's easily lost in distraction, and falls by the wayside to old patterns. To protect it, we need to do more. We need to set boundaries around what's meaningful so we can stay *aligned*, rather than buried beneath the constant pings of digital debris. Knowing what's important to you is just the beginning; now, you need to make the time and space to prioritise it.

As historian Will Durant distilled from the philosophies of Aristotle, 'We are what we repeatedly do.' To become the person you want to be, you need to consciously make decisions that *align to this identity daily*. You've chosen meaning—now, let's protect it.

14

ALIGN—Reframing Your Social Media Relationship

By now you can see more clearly what nourishes you, what provides you depth and what deeper needs you want to focus on. Maybe it's more connection, or maybe it's space for personal growth. Knowing this isn't enough; you need to create an environment where your expansion can be realised. You can do this by creating systems of *alignment*: structures that marry intention with action. The systems that hook you on chasing relevance still exist so, to avoid old patterns and prioritise the person you want to become, we will focus on setting boundaries: keeping out what no longer serves you, and protecting what matters.

After nearly 20 years of social media use, I had become so conditioned to picking up my phone and scrolling every few minutes that I didn't even realise I was doing it. My time and focus were so regularly being pulled into a web of distraction—I'd never stopped to consider if it was adding value to my life.

Social media had become a net-negative for me. It was well beyond intentional use—I was fully addicted. It had infiltrated every aspect of my life, from relationships to work. Not a single day went by without it.

At this point, I realised I no longer knew who I was without its influence.

The constant pings of notifications take a very real direct toll on our physiology. I was living in a state of *ambient stress*: low-level, persistent tension from being always 'on'. It's a hypervigilant, urgent state of endlessly checking, refreshing and responding.

Not only was this unsustainable for my nervous system, but it was also a distraction from being fully present in my own life. We can't reconnect to ourselves in this state. And this marks a new chapter in our journey—creating boundaries, which is the foundation of identity reclamation. It's *behavioural alignment.*

This is how we intentionally detach from our devices—for nominated periods, in specific spaces—so that our use becomes contained and controlled, rather than reactive and compulsive. Boundaries support our sense of agency and autonomy; by putting defined parameters around our use, we reclaim our time, space and energy—declaring where social media apps are no longer welcome.

Consider this your line in the sand. What you choose to do next has the power to change the direction of your life.

The taxonomy of boundaries

Boundaries are the fundamental first step in rewriting our relationship with social media. There's a growing body of research that shows the benefits of setting boundaries around social media and technology use, from reducing stress and boosting self-esteem to improving sleep quality and cognitive function.

But it's not as simple as just ditching all your apps cold turkey—trust me, I've tried. In our modern world, where technology is commonplace in our communication, communities and work lives, it's unrealistic to avoid it altogether. Instead, we need to invite more nuance. We need to reframe our relationship with it, rather than remove ourselves from it entirely. And we do this by setting clear and intentional boundaries that thoughtfully consider our unique needs.

These are the five different types of boundaries we'll use to do this:

1. Temporal boundaries
2. Spatial boundaries
3. Relational boundaries
4. Psychological boundaries
5. Content boundaries

1. *Temporal boundaries* are time-based boundaries with specific parameters around the time of day and the duration of time spent using social media.

They act as a circuit breaker to break dopamine-fuelled habit loops. They're also critical for regulating sleep, as research shows that checking social media close to bedtime leads to sleep disturbances, which ripple downstream and impact our cognition and decision making as a result. This makes us increasingly prone to making the wrong choices the following day.

What's more, research shows we consistently underestimate the amount of time we spend on devices. In short: we're subjectively poor at understanding our own habits and consistently think we use our phones less than we actually do.

Temporal boundaries lift the veil on our illusions. They expose our habits truthfully, helping us crack hard-to-break habit loops by creating space for us to reset the cycle.

2. *Spatial boundaries* are location-based boundaries that create physical distance from devices, such as spaces dedicated to being technology-free.

Science has long understood the role the environment plays in changing behaviour. For example, if you can't resist a drink, you might avoid bars, and if you like to gamble, you might avoid casinos. But how do we avoid a device that's always in our pocket?

Our phone comes everywhere with us, which means we need to be more deliberate about how we avoid its allure. Establishing device-free spaces—like bedrooms for rest, and office spaces for deep thinking—is imperative for creating physical distance from and diminishing reliance on our devices.

Spatial boundaries also expose our avoidance behaviours: the patterns that inhibit us from getting things done. My go-to avoidance behaviour is scrolling Instagram instead of responding to work emails, even though I know it won't resolve the problem. Avoidance behaviours offer temporary relief, while simultaneously ensuring the problem persists. Never once has scrolling made my emails disappear.

3. *Relational boundaries* are interpersonal relationship-based boundaries that protect our presence and interactions with others, while diminishing or removing the impact of negative people.

Relational boundaries protect the quality of our relationships. They help us carefully discern who receives our presence and who we need to reduce our exposure to. They help establish intentional investment in our relationships and a conscious awareness of who is influencing us.

They also reveal patterns harming the quality of our relationships, like *phubbing*—de-prioritising the person in front of you for your phone—which significantly decreases the quality of our relationships. In fact, the mere presence of a mobile phone can distract us during quality time with others.

What's more, we often follow people who annoy, frustrate or undermine us, unknowingly eroding our own self-worth and peace. When we expose ourselves to this content, we ensure that we'll feel worse-off after scrolling—and yet many of us can't resist.

Ultimately, relational boundaries ask two core questions:

- Who should I create stronger and deeper bonds with?
- Whose influence do I need to de-prioritise?

4. *Psychological boundaries* are mental and emotional boundaries that help us navigate our inner world through self-awareness, so we can better understand the impact of social media.

We know certain content is designed to manipulate our emotions and decision making, yet most of the time we're oblivious to this—doomscrolling without a second thought. Psychological boundaries ask us to become more attuned to our own inner experience. Exploring how we feel, what causes us to react and our resulting behaviour helps us calibrate the necessary boundaries to protect us from negative influence, especially in times of vulnerability.

Social media can quickly become a coping mechanism—a way to distract ourselves from boredom or numb uncomfortable emotions. But it is a temporary relief. We're bypassing meeting our actual needs: to develop the ability to acknowledge, process and self-regulate our emotions. And this dysregulation becomes a happy hunting ground for marketers and influencers alike, who are poised to exploit our weak moments by selling solutions promising to fill the void. A new outfit after a breakup. Fresh shoes following a stressful workday. Without psychological boundaries, our vulnerabilities can be more easily exploited on social media.

Psychological boundaries are a pause. They invite space for noticing and create our agency to respond rather than react. This reduces our dependency on consumeristic solutions to mental and emotional discomfort.

5. *Content boundaries* control the information we receive on our feed and reorient us towards values-aligned content with diversity of thought.

Content boundaries shape the mental environment we experience on social media. When we mindlessly scroll, we stop questioning what's appearing in our feed and why. We are consuming without awareness. What begins as curiosity can quickly become an echo chamber of algorithmic recommendations. Over time, this narrows our perspective and reinforces certain patterns of thinking and behaviour.

Content boundaries involve reflecting on what we're consuming and reorienting our feed so we are connecting to information, content and people that are values-aligned with us. They also encourage us to seek perspectives outside of social media to help reduce the influence of echo chambers and filter bubbles.

Content boundaries restore intention and broaden perspective for a more diverse worldview.

The following table provides a snapshot of how some of these boundaries might look, and why they work.

Boundary	Parameter	Examples	Why?	Benefits
Temporal	Time	• No phone before 9 am or after 7 pm • Screentime limits on apps • Screen-free periods (meals, family time)	Reduces fatigue, improves sleep and helps break habit loops	• Resets dopamine-fuelled habit loops • Improves circadian (sleep) rhythm • Reclaims time for nourishing activities
Spatial	Place	• No devices in the bedroom • Specific work/leisure-only zones • No phones at the dinner table	Supports ability to control focus, hold attention and break habit loops	• Create space for deep focus and attention • Removes distraction from certain environments • Prevents tech creep where you don't want it
Relational	Social	• Screen-free family/friend time • Muting/unfollowing people who undermine your self-worth • No phones during important conversations	Creates presence and connection in relationships, and creates distance from people with negative influence	• Supports bonding relationships • Increases oxytocin and serotonin release • Removes/diminishes interaction with negative sources • Improves empathy and genuine understanding of others

(continued)

Boundary	Parameter	Examples	Why?	Benefits
Psychological	Mind/ Emotions	• No scrolling when you're feeling vulnerable • Screens down if you get triggered before responding • Curating a diverse feed of things that inspire you	Restores agency when you're most susceptible to social media influence, thus minimising reactionary behaviour	• Improves self-awareness and emotional intelligence • Creates space to control reactive behaviour • Reorients attention into values-aligned content • Reduces social comparison and negative identity loops
Content	Information	• Limiting accounts with news and other anxiety-inducing information • Blocking toxic people/ influencers • Disabling algorithmic suggestions, such as saying no to 'ask app to track' requests • Not relying solely on social media for information (finding additional sources)	Reduces exposure to dark patterns from algorithms and echo chambers, and reorients you towards values-aligned content	• Restores personal agency over what you see • Broadens your worldview and access to diverse opinion • Improves overall emotional state and wellbeing

When I first decided to quit social media, I felt isolated and disconnected—out of the loop. But over time, the feeling transformed. In the absence of the noise, I started to feel things I hadn't for a long time: clarity, calm and connection. Finally, I was free from the hold it had over me.

But it wasn't without its challenges.

I was struggling to stay connected with friends and family abroad. I felt uninformed on many world issues. And it was a part of my work. Eventually (with trepidation), I decided to reintegrate it into my life—although this time, with purpose.

The hiatus had allowed me space. I felt clear about what matters most to me and how I could use social media differently.

It became a creative outlet, a source of inspiration and a vehicle to stay connected with the people who are important to me. Gone were the pseudo-connections, controversial celebrities, unqualified health 'experts' and creators, whose sole purpose is to provoke and polarise. Instead, I now follow authors, artists, musicians and podcasters who challenge and inspire how I think, which encourages growth.

Where previously social media had been a means to procrastinate and neglect uncomfortable real-life tasks, it soon became a carefully curated feed—one that I engage with at designated times, in allocated spaces and never in the presence of *real* companionship.

The change came from me, in the form of boundaries—I was *choosing* how I wanted to interact with these platforms.

You don't need to fully exclude yourself from social media to get the benefits of boundary setting. Instead, take a step back, audit your habits, reset your choices and implement boundaries to sustain them. This is how you rebuild your relationship with social media—one where you're in control.

Three steps for establishing digital boundaries

Boundaries support intentional social media use, allowing you to make decisions that protect what matters most to you. From awareness, through to alignment and action, we'll map this out together:

1. **Awareness:** Creating clarity on your social media habits, and their impact, is the foundation of change. It isn't until we understand this that we can make better-informed decisions. This clarity illuminates your current trajectory. In my journey, awareness was the single most powerful motivator for change: I didn't want to become a superficial, social-media-addicted shell of my full potential. I wanted to be in the driver's seat, owning my future and aligned to my vision.
2. **Alignment:** The clarity of awareness shows us where realignment is needed. To become a person you're proud of and leave a legacy that's uniquely yours, you need to remove the habits that aren't serving you and replace them with ones that do. And it's through creating boundaries that we build structure around that identity.
3. **Action:** The third piece is where awareness plus alignment becomes action. Setting boundaries helps to reinforce your identity and keep you accountable.

Together, these three steps become a framework that ensures your *identity* is central to your decision making, not social media.

Step 1: Awareness

All change begins with awareness. So, how are you using social media, really? It's time to get crystal clear on your habits. Awareness uncovers where your time and energy are going, and what that impact looks like.

Tracking your habits honestly is how we build awareness. To do this, we'll create a three-day log of your social media activity and how this impacts you. Essentially, it's just like journalling.

When I first did this for myself, I was shocked. My screentime painted a grim picture. Beyond that basic metric, when I journalled on my experience I became aware of the psychological, mental and spiritual toll this was taking. In particular, I felt ashamed of how little time I was spending with my family and friends—seemingly always too busy —and painfully aware that I had replaced this precious time with hours of doomscrolling.

But this exercise isn't about self-judgement—it's an opportunity. It's often not until we record our behaviour precisely that we uncover exactly what changes need to be made.

This is a personal check-in—it's an opportunity for awareness-building, not shaming or berating yourself. The more accurately and honestly you record your habits, the better informed you will be to make changes.

Begin with this exercise using the following framework (overleaf) before moving on to steps 2 and 3. This is an example log for one day; copy this table outline into your own journal and start recording. Continue this for three days, noting as many micro-moments as possible: these are crucial for understanding the volume of interruptions you encounter throughout the day, and their impact.

What	When	Where	With whom	For what purpose	How I felt
TikTok	First thing in the morning	From bed	Solo, random videos in my feed	Just because my phone was there	Buzzing, anxious, headache
Instagram	During my morning coffee	On the couch	My partner	Checking my feed	Distracted, anxious, bummed I had to go to work
Instagram	First opening computer for work	At my desk	Solo	No reason, just a habit	Distracted
TikTok	Around 10 am while checking emails	At my desk	Solo, random videos in feed	To check my feed while I checked my emails	Frustrated, scattered, anxious
Email	At work	At my desk	Solo	Reset inbox to check for new mail	Anticipation
Instagram	At work when I got an annoying email	At my desk	Solo	No reason, just a habit	Distracted, amused
Email	At work	At my desk	Solo	Got a ping	Excited, urgent
Instagram	During my lunch break	In the park	A friend from a nearby office	Checking my feed, sending memes to friends	Flat, distracted
YouTube	Around 4 pm	At my desk	Sent by a colleague via email	Watching a clip that had been sent to me	Guilty I wasn't working, amused, entertained
Instagram	Before the commute home	In my car	Solo	Checking my feed, sending memes to friends	Tired, bored, disconnected
Instagram	While making dinner	In the kitchen	My partner	Checking my feed, sending memes to friends	Tired, wired, anxious, not able to be present
YouTube	After dinner	On the couch	My partner	Watching some clips	Amused, entertained
Instagram	Lying in bed	In bed	My partner	Checking my feed, sending memes to friends	Tired, buzzing

Step 2: Alignment

With awareness comes a new question: 'Is this how I want to be living?'

My biggest fear when I quit social media was not knowing who I was without it—or whether anyone would still bother to contact me. After years of scrolling, posting and engaging, I'd lost touch with myself and the world offline. It had eroded my sense of self, and I was ready to discover what truly mattered without influence.

To do this, it's important to create time and space for deeper reflection. The prompts below will guide you and unpack more about your relationship with social media.

How you do this will look different for everyone. Perhaps you might like to meditate while you journal, or reflect while you take a walk outside. However you like to reflect, I encourage you to engage in that practice using the following prompts:

- Which platforms make me feel the most drained, and why?
- Where do I need to set boundaries to align with who I want to be?
- What parts of me do I feel pressure to perform on social media?
- What parts of me does it feel safer to keep hidden from social media?
- When no-one is watching (liking or commenting), who do I want to be and what do I value?
- What would need to change for me to lead with those values?

As you've learned in earlier chapters of this book, our self-concept becomes warped, and even lost, when we spend too much time on social media. From habit loops to algorithmic recommendations, our sense of self slowly disintegrates into a haze of influence.

The good news is that when our values and self-concept feel clearer and more defined, we're less susceptible to social comparison and its negative repercussions. This is why we step away from social media to get clarity, so we can re-engage on our terms.

With a clearer sense of who you want to be and what you value, you can now build boundaries to protect this—much like a moat or a wall—thus thwarting your reliance on social media and external validation to tell you who you are.

Step 3: Action

With your new-found clarity, you can now set values-aligned boundaries that reinforce this, rather than undermine who you are.

There are a few non-negotiable boundaries that I encourage you to adopt. This is because there's science-backed evidence showing they have positive outcomes for everyone, irrespective of our unique values and aspirations. These boundaries will support your overall wellbeing, sleep and relationships.

Setting boundaries takes a strong dose of *personal accountability*—they're only as good as your willingness to stick with them. And *you* are the only one responsible for this.

My advice is to start with one boundary in each of the five areas established earlier in this chapter. Be realistic, and start small. Stay firm for a short time period, and then celebrate your success with a non-technology reward at the end of the period. Don't reward yourself with an afternoon of doomscrolling! And don't make the reward disproportionate to your success—this will undermine your effort. For example, you might reward one week of no devices before bed or first-thing in the morning with a new book to read.

When it comes to new habit formation, it helps to pre-plan what you will do to replace the current habit—this ensures idle time doesn't lead to old patterns. For example, if you previously finished a stressful workday by scrolling TikTok on the couch, you might replace that behaviour with a 30-minute walk around your neighbourhood. This replacement behaviour helps you break the hold of the previous habit, while allowing a new habit to form. Starting small and sticking to it also boosts your confidence—and dopamine level—by proving to yourself you're capable of change.

Note: Don't throw the baby out with the bathwater if you slip up. While it's important to hold yourself accountable, know that you will inevitably slip along the way—so don't quit the entire process as a result. Treat each day as a new reset and the week as a milestone. It's like a social media streak, but offline. As you reach each milestone, reflect on what's working well and what's really challenging you—then recalibrate and repeat. This is how new habit loops are formed.

Setting your boundaries: The two non-negotiables

Certain boundaries are universally beneficial. Here are two non-negotiable boundaries I challenge you to accept because science has proven them to be healthy for all of us:

- No phones or devices for the first and last hour before bed every day (temporal boundary).

  Recommended replacement: Reading for 30 minutes before bed and when you first wake up.
- No phones or devices inside the bedroom (spatial boundary).

  Recommended replacement: Use an analogue alarm clock (no smart features) to wake up.

There is ample evidence that screens before bed have a detrimental impact on our circadian rhythm and sleep quality—and your sleep quality is crucial to your ability to make wise decisions. In moments when we feel tired, low in energy and mentally fatigued, we're most vulnerable to falling into old patterns of behaviour.

Here are some examples of how the remaining boundaries might look.

Type	Boundary	Replacement behaviour	Milestone
Relational boundary	No phones or devices during meals and while people are speaking to you.	Each person at the table shares their favourite moment from the day.	One week
Psychological boundary	When I am upset, triggered or anxious I put the phone down and walk away for 15 minutes.	When I am upset, triggered or anxious I put the phone down and take a 15-minute walk around the neighbourhood. OR When I am upset, triggered or anxious I put the phone down, take five deep breaths and write down how I'm feeling.	One week
Content boundary	Disable algorithmic suggestions from all social media platforms.	Explore a new interest offline such as reading an interesting book, joining a club or taking a class.	One week

Once awareness and alignment are established, it's time to take action (see figure 14.1). When you start small and begin implementing your boundaries, it's important to assess how effective they are at the end of your chosen milestone periods. This deepens your awareness further and allows you to recalibrate to keep moving forward.

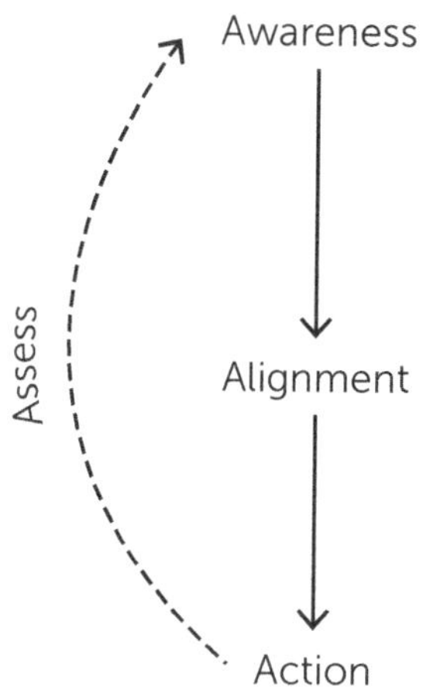

Figure 14.1 How setting boundaries to create space to reclaim your identity looks in action.

Some questions to consider when setting your boundaries:

- Are there times of the day when you would like more rest? What activities feel restful (for example, reading, walking, painting), and how can you eliminate devices to make space for that chunk of time each day?
- Are there content creators, influencers or even friends who seem to trigger you more than others?
- Could you create a technology-free space where you can go to think deeply, relax or engage in a hobby?
- Are there relationships I would like to focus more time and energy into, in person?

The hard truth: Change *is* hard—at first

When we first choose to do anything differently, it feels hard at first. This is because we experience *mental friction*: the resistance that often comes in the form of thoughts like 'this is too hard' when we first embark on a change. Mental friction occurs because your brain is trying harder than usual to do the new thing, rather than repeating an old and familiar pattern. This is just your brain's response to creating new neural pathways—it is not a sign of weakness or wrongness, and you should persist through the friction.

Everything new feels hard, before it feels easy. But the only person who can make the change is you, and over time these new habits will begin to feel easy, too.

Your mind may try to convince you the old ways are better, because they're easier—but don't believe everything you think. These are just old stories that don't serve the *future you.* Here are a few lies I told myself at first, and how I resolved them:

- I need my phone for my morning alarm. *I bought an alarm clock instead.*
- I use my phone to tell the time. *I wore a watch.*
- I need my phone with me in case of an emergency. *I installed a landline and let people know when I wasn't contactable (such as 'I'm going hiking, I'll be back in two hours').*
- I need social media to contact my friends. *I gave them my number. If you're friends, they'll call (this one was a hard truth to swallow).*

With your renewed clarity and boundaries, it's time to road-test them. It helps to remember the science behind why we're starting small with just one boundary each over a week—it's called *behavioural activation*: small changes start shifting our identity, and as we feel those changes we start to feel increased self-belief. Momentum and motivation follow actions. This is how you form a new, positive habit —start doing the thing, feel better as a result, believe you can do it, then repeat.

Remember, change is about becoming who you want to be—it's not just about becoming more productive. Ask yourself: 'If I can reclaim my attention, what might that mean for who I want to become?'

15

LIVE—A Life That You Belong To

Here's what this book has been building towards: supporting you to remember that creating a life that feels true to yourself is within your reach. You don't need to quit technology forever and move to a cabin in the woods to achieve this. Instead, you can integrate technology into your life in a way that works for you and doesn't give it free reign to dictate.

Many of us feel like passengers to our social media habits, but what we want is to feel in control. In a world that profits from our distraction, comparison and compulsion to perform, we've forgotten what it's like to step off the hamster wheel and really live on our own terms. This is an invitation to choose differently—to choose depth and presence over pseudo-connection. To think deeply and autonomously for yourself. To choose meaning and contribution over visibility and performance. And, ultimately, to define the legacy you'll someday leave behind.

This has never just been about social media. Instead, it's an exploration of what happens when we allow constant influence to tell us what to wear, how to act, what to think and *who we should be*. Being *real* is now a modern act of *rebellion*. And as you wade out of the haze of influence, you return to a place of alignment. You return home—to the *real* you.

The most profound realisation I had, through the journey of untangling myself from social media, was recognising how little time I'd spent thinking about my future. Lost in the fray of constant distraction and instant validation, I had been unconsciously sabotaging my own future. The trajectory I was on didn't align with the person I wanted to be, or the legacy I wanted to leave behind. My fixation with trends and influencer content had come at the expense of planting any seeds that would support me to grow into the person I wanted to become. This was the moment I decided to reclaim my agency and make changes.

We have explored how social media distorts our identity, influences the decisions we make, impacts our relationships, and even harms our mental health and wellbeing. We've also examined the social media mechanisms behind this. But this awareness alone doesn't drive change. It's now time to ask yourself the hard question: 'Who am I becoming through what I repeatedly do?' Because whether you're consciously choosing this or not, you are *always* becoming *someone.*

What you pay attention to, who you garner influence from and how you use social media isn't just a way to fill your time—it fundamentally shapes your identity, and your life. And when we aren't paying attention, we become a version of ourselves we no longer recognise. Beyond just shaping who we are right now, our digital selves also leave breadcrumbs for how others will ultimately remember us.

Before we can look forward, it's important we reflect honestly. Which is why it's useful to begin by reflecting on our digital legacy to date, then evaluating if it paints a picture of a person we're proud of. From there, we'll explore how to realign our behaviour so we can sustainably move towards being the person we want to be.

This chapter is practical. So please bring a pen, some paper and a willingness to deep dive into the work before you move on.

Clarity: The identity you leave behind

Treat this moment like the end of one chapter of your life, and the beginning of a new one. There's the version of you—the one shaped by habits, influence and algorithms—that's brought you to this point. And there's a version of you that's still becoming.

To move forward with clarity and intention, we need to first reflect on what your current digital identity says about you.

The current version of me

Honestly, without judgement, take time to answer the following.

In a notepad or journal, slowly reflect on the following prompts and *write* (not type) your answers.

1. If a stranger saw my social media, what would they learn about me?
2. If I looked back on my digital identity at 80, would I be proud of what I see?
3. If someone saw only my last 10 posts, what would they assume I care about most?
4. Does this reflect what I want to be known for?

Now, go a little deeper. Audit your current behaviour against who you want to become—the *future* you.

To do this, divide your page into three columns:

- **Column A:** Behaviours I'm leaving in the past. What parts of your digital identity do you need to leave behind?
- **Column B:** Behaviours I'm continuing into the future. What parts feel grounded, aligned and worth carrying forward?

(continued)

- **Column C:** Important parts of my identity that are missing online. What feels meaningful and real, offline, that's missing from my online identity?

Here's my personal example below:

Behaviours I'm leaving in the past	**Behaviours I'm continuing into the future**	**Important parts of my identity that are missing online**
Commenting impulsively or sarcastically	Thoughtfully commenting on posts to show my support	My creative projects, like poetry, that I've been too afraid to share
Following influencers who make me feel unworthy	Following people who inspire me to grow and expand	My sense of humour that people value in real life, but I don't show online
Only sharing selfies when I look good	Sharing photographs from my travels and things that inspire me	My volunteer work—I volunteer at the aged care centre but no-one knows this about me
Using social media as a way to procrastinate	Using social media to intentionally connect and learn	Sharing more content that aligns to my values, like kindness and service
Sharing 'hot takes' to stir engagement and feel relevant	Writing thoughtful posts about what I really believe in, even if it gets minimal likes	Using my lived experience to connect with others through my writing
Comparing myself to others	Celebrating my own milestones, big or small	My deeper friendships, family and connections
Lurking and passively watching others' lives via Stories	Engaging in online communities that fill my cup	My music community, which I've recently become a part of, but because I'm still learning have been too afraid to share

Reflecting on your answers, consider:

- Why do I feel ready to leave these behaviours behind?
- How will the behaviours I want to continue contribute positively to my future?
- How might it look to start integrating the missing parts of myself online?

This is where rewriting your digital legacy begins—with intentional and aligned congruence between who you want to become and how you reinforce this through your online behaviour.

Connection: Creating a bridge to your future self

Through his decades of research, psychologist and author Hal Hershfield found that when we feel more connected with, and positive about, our future self, we're more inclined to make decisions that benefit that future identity today. For example, we're more likely to save money for retirement, eat healthier and make decisions that support our future self when we feel a sense of *connection* to that future identity.

However, this future vision often feels abstract and out of reach—a distant figment or dream rather than a *continuity* of who we are now. As a result, we don't make decisions in our own best interests; instead, we default to old patterns and make things easier here and now, unknowingly sabotaging our vision. This is what it looks like to stay *stuck*. Over time, these small and seemingly inconsequential choices accumulate, determining who we become.

This is where we close the gap. By creating a sense of continuity between who you are now and who you're becoming, you translate your intention into clear actions.

Future self-reflection

Find a quiet space. Grab your journal, or a blank piece of paper. Take a deep breath. Now imagine yourself 10 years from now, living in a way that feels deeply genuine:

- Where are you waking up and how are you feeling?
- What kind of work, creative pursuits and hobbies feel most meaningful?
- Who do you spend time with that makes you feel grounded and understood?
- What gives you a sense of peace, joy and pride?
- Where do you find fun, pleasure and playfulness?
- What does your relationship with technology look like?

Now, write a letter from that future self to your present self. Give them advice on:

- What did you stop doing that changed everything?
- What are you grateful you started doing?
- What helped you to stay focused, even in a world full of distraction?
- What's the one thing you want your present self to prioritise?

You're not just finding clarity and connection; you're building psychological flexibility. As you connect to your future self, you begin to see you're not stuck right now; instead, you're capable of change and reinvention, and there are many paths that can take you there.

You have the opportunity to make decisions now that will bring this vision to life.

Continuity: Rituals for becoming

Through the clarity of awareness, and connection that creates direction, you now understand who you want to become and why. *Continuity* is where you build the rituals that create and sustain this change. This is where inspiration shifts into tangible, repeatable habits and behaviours that reinforce who you want to become. This is what you *choose* to repeatedly do to bring your future self into reality.

Rituals aren't about rigidity or restriction; instead, they provide anchors to the person you're becoming. They are small, consistent acts of discipline—the ultimate form of self-care—moving you forward with intention. Your rituals guide you away from old patterns and towards a new trajectory.

If clarity is your foundation, and connection is the structure, then continuity is what makes the house liveable. This is what makes a house feel like a *home*—through the maintenance, warmth and light you bring to your rituals, your future self becomes something you *live* every day. Continuity allows you to *inhabit* this vision and transform your ideas into the embodiment of your everyday lived experience.

In Chapter 3, we reflected on how our digital identity is just one fragment of our whole self. Using the cake analogy, our digital self is one slice—the rest of us is what makes up the whole (delicious!) thing. And, like any recipe, the right amount of each ingredient is needed for success.

Building rituals that support your growth and thriving require you to tend to the different parts of yourself. From your inner world to your career, relationships to play, these rituals underpin all that's important to us to ensure we're nourishing ourselves in all the different ways we need.

This process is two-step: First, we'll get clear on who you want to become across all the different parts of yourself, then we'll create rituals that prioritise these accordingly—ensuring you're investing your time and energy in ways that positively contribute towards your future self.

Here are the six different domains we'll use to guide this reflection (see also figure 15.1):

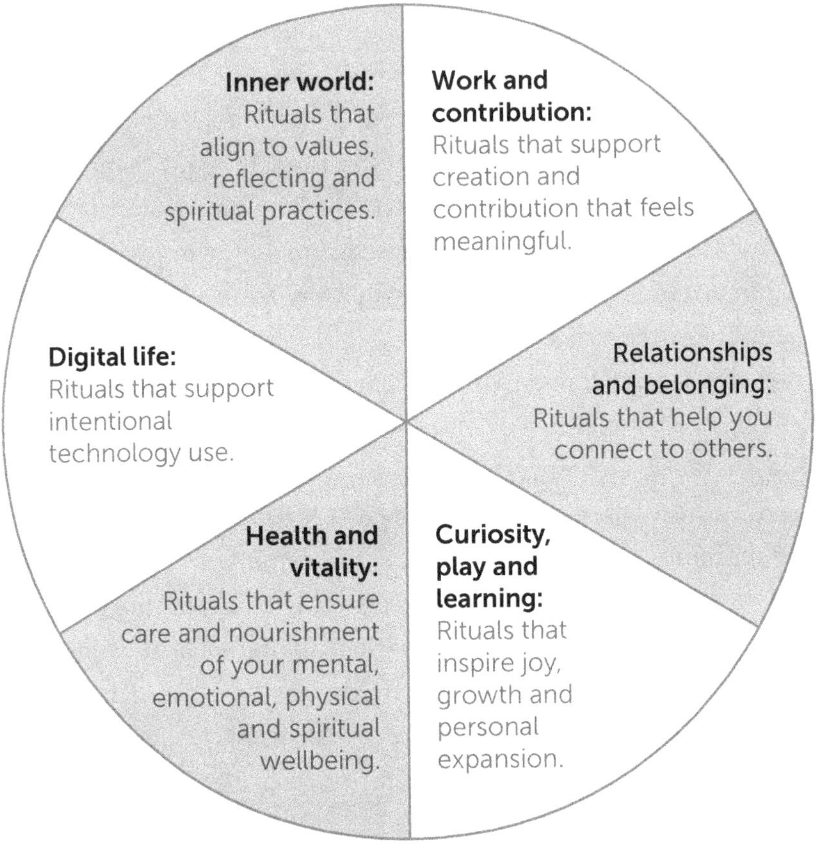

Figure 15.1 Creating a blueprint for rituals that support our vision of our future self.

- **Inner world:** Rituals that align to values, reflecting and spiritual practices
- **Work and contribution:** Rituals that support creation and contribution that feels meaningful

- **Relationships and belonging:** Rituals that help you connect to others
- **Curiosity, play and learning:** Rituals that inspire joy, growth and personal expansion
- **Health and vitality:** Rituals that ensure care and nourishment of your mental, emotional, physical and spiritual wellbeing
- **Digital life:** Rituals that support intentional technology use

Two steps towards building continuity through rituals

Step 1: Future self identity markers

With clarity on who you want to become, connecting rituals to these identity markers across the six different domains helps create sustainable and 'sticky' habits. As James Clear explored in *Atomic Habits*, when our habits are rooted in identity rather than goal attainment, they become about progress rather than success—and this is what makes them sustainable for the long haul.

Reflecting on each of the six domains, consider the type of person you want to become in each. We'll turn these reflections into statements about your identity, rather than goals, so they feel like something you can continually journey towards.

Begin with the statement, 'My future self is someone who...' as you consider each domain. Here are my statements:

- **Inner world:**...prioritises quiet reflection and downtime *(not scrolling)*
- **Work and contribution:**...uses my time to create things that feel meaningful and are important to me *(rather than just consuming)*

(continued)

- **Relationships and belonging:**...spends quality time with people who light me up, challenge me and make me feel understood *(rather than online connections and influencers)*
- **Curiosity, play and learning:**...protects my time and attention for things that excite me and bring me new insight *(rather than wasting time doomscrolling or creating content that doesn't add value to my life)*
- **Health and vitality:**...prioritises my health by staying active and sleeping routinely *(rather than allowing social media to hijack my downtime and sleep patterns)*
- **Digital life:**...shares my creative endeavours proudly online *(rather than just consuming content on creative endeavours I admire)*.

Try these for yourself without rushing. Sit with them, take your time and truly connect to what feels meaningful for you.

Step 2: Building rituals to reinforce identity

For each identity statement from Step 1, create one small, repeatable ritual. These aren't aspirational statements—they need to be realistic. These rituals will be reinforced by the boundaries you established in Chapter 14.

For example (using my statements from Step 1):

- If your future self prioritises quiet reflection and downtime, start the morning with 10 minutes of journalling while enjoying your coffee alone.
- If your future self uses their time to create things that feel meaningful and important, volunteer once a month at the local library, sporting club or aged care home.

- If your future self spends quality time with people who light them up, challenge them and make them feel understood, grab a coffee every Friday morning with a different friend.
- If your future self protects their time and attention for things that light them up and spark insight, take guitar lessons biweekly to build a new skill you've always admired.
- If your future self prioritises health by staying active and sleeping routinely, take a walk every day after work in your local park to wind down from the day.
- If your future self shares their creative endeavours proudly online, ask yourself before posting anything, 'Is this expression or performance?'

You don't become your future self all at once. Yet, over time, as you repeat these rituals time and again, they become your everyday reality. Repeated over a month, over a year, throughout a decade, they become your future self—no longer a distant dream, but your lived reality.

This is how you become who you've always known you could be.

Epilogue: Looking to the Future

You've made it: not just to the end of this book, but to the beginning of a new chapter in your life—one that's deeper and richer in meaning, and where you're in the driver's seat. You've peeled back the layers of performance, identity, validation and habit to meet yourself where you are—and recalibrate who you want to be moving forward. You've reconnected to the *real* you.

Social media will remain an integral part of modern life, but now you're equipped with the framework and tools to stay aligned to what matters most, without social media hijacking your journey.

When I undertook this journey for myself it was like opening Pandora's box. I knew once I started asking the hard questions of myself, an existential crisis would follow—and I'm glad it did. Without the courage to ask ourselves the uncomfortable and revealing questions, we don't illuminate the parts of ourselves where growth and expansion is possible.

I still use social media. Despite having drastically shifted my online habits so that they complement my goals and real-life relationships, there are still days where I struggle with its influence. There are times I still find myself doomscrolling, getting triggered, and believing people and 'facts' when I should know better—but with these tools, I can support myself in these situations, which you can do, too.

I've also built incredible relationships with people I've met online. From starting a business and a podcast with an online contact, to finding incredible mentors from around the world on my writing journey, I've shifted my social media habits so they add value to my life rather than subtract from my experiences. And this is something we all have the power to do.

You now understand that:

- Attention isn't just a resource—it's your fundamental *life force.*
- Who you are isn't found in tiny squares on a screen —it's built from *within.*
- Social media validation isn't a form of connection—that comes when we truly *bond.*
- Meaning isn't relevance—it's a deeper *expression of self.*
- To reconnect to the real you, you need to be willing to *Realise, Expand, Align and Live.*

Don't be fooled: integrating these practices, boundaries and rituals to prioritise a meaningful life takes courage—the courage to step away from the endless noise and expectations blasted at us from every inch of the internet. But when we do this, life becomes richer, deeper and worth far more than a follower count.

You'll still scroll. You'll still get stuck on the surface. And you'll still compare yourself to the idealised world of social media. But when you do, there's always the choice to put your phone down and reconnect with your future self, gently reminding yourself that you're the creator of meaning, not just content.

Keep asking yourself the hard question: 'Am I living a life I feel proud to live?'

I'm cheering for you, in *real* time.

Glossary

Algorithmic curation The process by which digital platforms use algorithms to filter and prioritise the content users see, shaping perceptions and behaviours.

Attention economy A system where human attention is treated as a commodity, competed for by platforms, brands and media outlets.

Context collapse The merging of multiple audiences (friends, colleagues, family) into one undifferentiated audience on social media, often leading to self-censorship or performance.

Digital boundaries Limits individuals set to manage online behaviour, protect wellbeing and prevent digital overreach into their personal lives.

Echo chamber An environment—often online—where you encounter information and opinions that mirror your own; as a result, this leads to the reinforcement and amplification of your existing beliefs, while excluding opposing views.

Eudaimonic wellbeing A deeper sense of flourishing based on meaning, growth and alignment with values, contrasted with short-term pleasure (hedonic wellbeing).

Filter bubble An environment created by algorithms that exposes individuals only to similar content.

FOMO (fear of missing out) The anxious feeling that others are having rewarding experiences without you, which is heightened by social media feeds.

Future self A psychological concept describing how imagining oneself in the future can influence present-day decision making and wellbeing.

Genuine connection Relationships characterised by genuineness, reciprocity and presence, often contrasted with shallow or pseudo-connection online.

Genuine fake paradox The paradox of seeking authenticity in digital spaces while inevitably performing and curating for an audience, which lead to identities that are simultaneously real and fabricated.

Habit loop A behavioural cycle of cue, craving, response, reward that reinforces patterns, including digital habits like checking notifications.

Hedonic wellbeing Wellbeing derived from pleasure, comfort and avoidance of pain, which is often short-lived (contrasted with eudaimonic wellbeing).

Parasocial relationship A one-sided bond where a follower feels emotionally connected to a media figure, influencer or celebrity who is unaware of their existence.

Phubbing Snubbing someone in person by prioritising attention to a phone or device (a term coined by McCann, an Australian advertising agency in 2012).

Profile self The version of self that is constructed and performed through digital platforms, often curated to align with desired perceptions.

Pseudo-connection Superficial connections formed online that mimic, but do not fully replace, genuine, offline relationships.

Self-objectification Viewing oneself as an object to be evaluated based on appearance or social approval, which is often reinforced by social media.

Social comparison The process of evaluating oneself in relation to others, which is often intensified by curated social media feeds.

System 1 thinking Fast, intuitive and automatic processing that is prone to bias and error.

System 2 thinking Slow, deliberate and analytical reasoning that requires conscious effort.

Acknowledgements

It'd be remiss not to mention the person who's made this dream possible first and foremost. To my partner Ryan, who's quietly stood beside me this entire process, there were more moments than I can count where I needed to lean into his belief in me before I could believe in myself. Without needing to ask, he's picked up the slack in every way—from ensuring there's always a meal on the table when I write late to a lunch packed ready for when I'm inevitably late for work again, and everything in between. Having a partner that sees you, and sees your potential, can't be overstated. Not only have you made this dream possible for me, but you make life infinitely better. I love you, and thank you.

To my mum Janet, and brother Callan—who actually had no idea I was writing a book until the initial draft was complete—thank you for your excitement, belief and support. Knowing I was the proud topic of conversation at many bowlo gatherings was my true motivation for writing this. I know this would have made Dad proud, too.

It truly takes a village, so thanks—in no particular order—to some of my village: Sally Clarke, Amy Easton, Susan Perrow, Martin Gutmann PhD, Dr Delia McCabe, Professor Hans Georg-Moeller and Dr Amy Finlay-Jones. Thank you for your words of wisdom, support, friendship, mentorship, expert insight and everything in between. Each one of you played a role in this journey.

To the whole team at Wiley, in particular my commissioning editor, Jordon Lott, thank you for seeing the value in my book and taking this project on. To say I'm grateful isn't near enough.

And last, but not least, I want to thank me for seeing myself through the hardest undertaking of my life to produce a resource I wish I'd had 20 years ago.

Reader Companion Guide

If you loved this book and would like to read more on some of the topics included here, here are some of the books, Substack pages and other resources that have inspired me.

On influence, authenticity and performance

Robert Cialdini – Influence

Why read it: The classic guide to persuasion and why we say 'yes' more often than we think—from marketing to social media likes.

Erving Goffman – The Presentation of Self in Everyday Life

Why read it: Written long before Instagram, this sociological gem explains why life is a stage—online or off.

Emily Hund – The Influencer Industry: The quest for authenticity on social media

Why read it: Explores how 'authenticity' became a commodity in the digital age, tracing the rise of influencers and the commercialisation of selfhood.

Hans-Georg Moeller and Paul D'Ambrosio – You and Your Profile

Why read it: A deep dive into why 'authenticity' online feels slippery—and how profiles have changed what identity means.

Hans-Georg Moeller and Paul D'Ambrosio – Genuine Pretending

Why read it: Offers a refreshing alternative to the Western obsession with being 'true to yourself', drawn from Chinese philosophy.

Jia Tolentino – Trick Mirror

Why read it: Witty, sharp essays on self-delusion, Instagram culture, and what it means to perform our lives.

On habits, disconnection and attention

James Clear – Atomic Habits

Why read it: A toolkit for breaking unhelpful loops and building habits that actually stick—essential in a world designed for distraction.

Johann Hari – Stolen Focus

Why read it: A timely look at why our attention spans are shrinking—and how reclaiming focus is key to deeper living.

Johann Hari – Lost Connections

Why read it: A compassionate exploration of why we feel lonely and disconnected, and what really brings us back to meaning.

Dr Delia McCabe – The State of the Modern Mind (Substack)

Why read it: Explores how modern lifestyles, diet, and digital overwhelm shape brain health—and what we can do to restore clarity and focus.

On identity and misinformation

Matthew Facciani—Misguided: Where misinformation starts, how it spreads, and what to do about it

Why read it: A compelling look at how misinformation spreads and why it's so hard to change minds—crucial for navigating today's information chaos.

Jennifer Forestal—In the age of cancel culture, shaming can be healthy for online communities—a political scientist explains when and how (article, *The Conversation*)

Why read it: An important guide on how we can interact in digital spaces to drive connection and understanding rather than division when we disagree with others.

On comparison, beauty and body image

Heather Widdows – Perfect Me

Why read it: A bold exploration of beauty as a moral ideal—and why it's so hard to escape its pull in a filtered world.

On future selves, flourishing and provocation

Kate Gustin – The No-Self Help Book

Why read it: A liberating take on identity, showing how letting go of the 'self' can actually help us live more freely.

Jonathan Haidt – The Happiness Hypothesis

Why read it: A blend of ancient wisdom and modern psychology—a roadmap to meaning that feels timeless in a world chasing relevance.

Jonathan Haidt – The Anxious Generation

Why read it: Explores how the shift to an all-digital childhood has fuelled a crisis in mental health—vital context for parents, educators and anyone navigating Gen Z's digital landscape.

Todd Kashdan – Provoked (Substack)

Why read it: A refreshing, sometimes uncomfortable, but always thought-provoking take on living courageously—perfect for readers who want to turn discomfort into growth.

References

Chapter 1

Cooley, CH (1902). *Human Nature and the Social Order*. Scribner's.

Goffman, E (1959). *The Presentation of Self in Everyday Life*. Anchor Books.

Rosa, H (2013). *Social Acceleration: A New Theory of Modernity*. Columbia University Press.

Chapter 2

Cialdini, RB (2009). *Influence: The psychology of persuasion*. HarperCollins.

Fredrickson, BL and Roberts, T-A (1997). Objectification theory: Toward understanding women's lived experiences and mental health risks. *Psychology of Women Quarterly*, 21(2), 173–206. https://doi.org/10.1111/j.1471-6402.1997.tb00108.x

Moradi, B and Huang, Y-P (2008). Objectification theory and psychology of women: A decade of advances and future directions. *Psychology of Women Quarterly*, 32(4), 377–398. https://doi.org/10.1111/j.1471-6402.2008.00452.x

Tiggemann, M and Slater, A (2014). NetGirls: The Internet, Facebook, and body image concern in adolescent girls. *International Journal of Eating Disorders*, 47(6), 630–643. https://doi.org/10.1002/eat.22141

Tolentino, J (2019). *Trick Mirror: Reflections on self-delusion*. Random House.

Tolentino, J (2019). The age of Instagram face. *The New Yorker*.

Widdows, H (2018). *Perfect me: Beauty as an ethical ideal*. Princeton University Press.

Chapter 3

Fardouly, J, Diedrichs, PC, Vartanian, LR and Halliwell, E (2015). Social comparisons on social media: The impact of Facebook on young women's body image concerns and mood. *Body Image,* 13, 38–45. https://doi.org/10.1016/j.bodyim.2014.12.002

Festinger, L (1954). A theory of social comparison processes. *Human Relations,* 7(2), 117–140. https://doi.org/10.1177/001872675400700202

Higgins, ET (1987). Self-discrepancy: A theory relating self and affect. *Psychological Review,* 94(3), 319–340. https://doi.org/10.1037/0033-295X.94.3.319

Linville, PW (1987). Self-complexity as a cognitive buffer against stress-related illness and depression. *Journal of Personality and Social Psychology,* 52(4), 663–676. https://doi.org/10.1037/0022-3514.52.4.663

Vogel, EA, Rose, JP, Roberts, LR and Eckles, K (2014). Social comparison, social media, and self-esteem. *Psychology of Popular Media Culture,* 3(4), 206–222. https://doi.org/10.1037/ppm0000047

Yee, N and Bailenson, J (2007). The Proteus effect: The effect of transformed self-representation on behavior. *Human Communication Research,* 33(3), 271–290. https://doi.org/10.1111/j.1468-2958.2007.00299.x

Chapter 4

Ebben, M and Bull, E (2023). *Constructing authenticity: Social media influencers and the shaping of online identity.* In Online Identity*: An essential guide.* IntechOpen. https://doi.org/10.5772/intechopen.1002607

Hund, E (2023). *The Influencer Industry: The quest for authenticity on social media.* Princeton University Press.

Kernis, MH and Goldman, BM (2006). A multicomponent conceptualization of authenticity: Theory and research. *Advances in Experimental Social Psychology,* 38, 283–357. https://doi.org/10.1016/S0065-2601(06)38006-9

Moeller, H-G and D'Ambrosio, P (2017). *Genuine Pretending: On the philosophy of the Zhuangzi.* Columbia University Press.

Moeller, H-G and D'Ambrosio, P (2021). *You and Your Profile: Identity after authenticity.* Columbia University Press.

Park, RE (1950). *Race and Culture.* Free Press.

Purser, R (2019). *McMindfulness: How mindfulness became the new capitalist spirituality.* Repeater.

Tappin, B and McKay, R (2016). The Illusion of Moral Superiority. *Social Psychological and Personality Science,* 8(6), 623–631. https://doi.org/10.1177/1948550616673878

Chapter 5

Alberta Health Services (2025). *Problematic use of digital technology – Screening and assessment tools* (Youth Addiction and Mental Health Guide).

Amirthalingam, J and Khera, A (2024). Understanding social media addiction: A deep dive. *Cureus,* 16(10), e72499. https://doi.org/10.7759/cureus.72499

Andreassen, CS, Pallesen, S and Griffiths, MD (2017). The relationship between addictive use of social media, narcissism, and self-esteem: Findings from a large national survey. *Addictive Behaviors,* 64, 287–293. https://doi.org/10.1016/j.addbeh.2016.03.006

Berridge, KC, Robinson, TE and Aldridge, JW (2009). Dissecting components of reward: 'Liking', 'wanting', and learning. *Current Opinion in Pharmacology,* 9(1), 65–73. https://doi.org/10.1016/j.coph.2008.12.014

Boer, M, Stevens, GWJM, Finkenauer, C, *et al* (2022). Validation of the Social Media Disorder Scale in adolescents: Findings from a large-scale nationally representative sample. *Assessment,* 29(8), 1658–1675. https://doi.org/10.1177/10731911211027232

Clear, J (2018). *Atomic Habits: An easy and proven way to build good habits and break bad ones.* Avery.

Haidt, J and Lukianoff, G (2018). *The Coddling of the American Mind: How good intentions and bad ideas are setting up a generation for failure.* Penguin.

Moretta T and Wegmann E (2025). Toward the classification of social media use disorder: Clinical characterization and proposed diagnostic criteria. *Addictive Behaviors Reports,* 21, 100603. https://doi.org/10.1016/j.abrep.2025.100603

Skinner, BF (1948). 'Superstition' in the pigeon. *Journal of Experimental Psychology,* 38(2), 168–172. https://doi.org/10.1037/h0055873

Wise, RA and Jordan, CJ (2021). Dopamine, behavior, and addiction. *Journal of Biomedical Science,* 28, 83. https://doi.org/10.1186/s12929-021-00779-7

Young, KS (1998). Internet addiction: The emergence of a new clinical disorder. *Cyberpsychology and Behavior,* 1(3), 237–244. https://doi.org/10.1089/cpb.1998.1.237

Chapter 6

Altmann, EM, Trafton, JG and Hambrick, DZ (2014). Momentary interruptions can derail the train of thought. *Journal of Experimental Psychology General*, 143(1), 215–226. https://doi.org/10.1037/a0030986

American Psychological Association (2006). Multitasking: Switching costs. https://www.apa.org/topics/research/multitasking

Busylight.com (n.d.). Reducing workplace stress: How status indicators lower interruption anxiety. https://busylight.com/reducing-workplace-stress-how-status-indicators-lower-interruption-anxiety/

Chis, M, Li, H, Zheng, K *et al* (2023). The cognitive load—productivity tradeoff in task switching. *Proceedings of the Human Factors and Ergonomics Society Annual Meeting*, 67(1), 666–671.

Deschamps, A, Fortier, M-È, Muñoz Gómez, N, *et al* (2025). Understanding phubbing behavior: A scoping review of qualitative and mixed-methods studies. *Computers in Human Behavior Reports*, 18, 100684. https://doi.org/10.1016/j.chbr.2025.100684

Drinko, C (2026). The dark side of phubbing. *Psychology Today*.

Hari, J (2022). *Stolen Focus: Why you can't pay attention—and how to think deeply again*. Bloomsbury Publishing.

Katidioti, I, Borst, J, van Vugt, M and Taatgen, N (2016). Interrupt me: External interruptions are less disruptive than self-interruptions. *Computers in Human Behavior*, 63, 906–915. https://doi.org/10.1016/j.chb.2016.06.037

Murty, RN, Dadlani, S and Das, RB (2022). How much time and energy do we waste toggling Between applications? *Harvard Business Review*.

Newport, C (2019). *Digital minimalism: Choosing a focused life in a noisy world*. Portfolio.

Ni, N, Ahrari, S, Zaremohzzabieh, Z, Zarean, M and Roslan, S (2025). A meta-analytic study of partner phubbing and its antecedents and consequences. *Frontiers in Psychology*, 16, 1561159. https://doi.org/10.3389/fpsyg.2025.1561159

Mark, G (2023). *Attention Span: A Groundbreaking Way to Restore Balance,* Happiness and Productivity. Hanover Square Press.

Turkle, S (2011). *Alone Together: Why we expect more from technology and less from each other*. Basic Books.

Chapter 7

Baumeister, RF (1982). A self-presentational view of social phenomena. *Psychological Bulletin*, 91(1), 3–26. https://doi.org/10.1037/0033-2909.91.1.3

Baumeister, RF and Leary, MR (1995). The need to belong: Desire for interpersonal attachments as a fundamental human motivation. *Psychological Bulletin*, 117(3), 497–529. https://doi.org/10.1037/0033-2909.117.3.497

Baumeister, RF and Vohs, KD (Eds). (2004). *Handbook of Self-Regulation: Research, theory, and applications*. Guilford Press.

Cross, RL and Dillon, K (2023). *The Microstress Effect: How little things pile up and create big problems—and what to do about it*. Harvard Business Review Press.

McGinnis, PJ (2004). *Social theory at HBS: McGinnis' two FOs. The Harbus.*

Chapter 8

Amalia, A (2025). Content formats: What Gen Z wants vs. millennials. *ContentGrip*. https://www.contentgrip.com/gen-z-wants-vs-millennials-content-formats/

Center for Countering Digital Hate (2022). *The disinformation dozen: Why platforms must act on twelve leading online anti-vaxxers*. https://counterhate.com/research/the-disinformation-dozen/

The Decision Lab (n.d.). Illusory truth effect. https://thedecisionlab.com/biases/illusory-truth-effect

Facciani, M (2025). *Misguided: Where misinformation starts, how it spreads, and what to do about it*. Columbia University Press.

Forestal, J (2024). In the age of cancel culture, shaming can be healthy for online communities—a political scientist explains when and how. *The Conversation*. https://theconversation.com/in-the-age-of-cancel-culture-shaming-can-be-healthy-for-online-communities-a-political-scientist-explains-when-and-how-221730

Hasher, L, Goldstein, D and Toppino, T (1977). Frequency and the conference of referential validity. *Journal of Verbal Learning and Verbal Behavior*, 16(1), 107–112. https://doi.org/10.1016/S0022-5371(77)80012-1

Keltner, D (1996). Evidence for the distinctness of embarrassment, shame, and guilt: A study of recalled antecedents and facial expressions of emotion. *Cognition and Emotion*, 10(2), 155–172. https://doi.org/10.1080/026999396380312

Marwick, AE (2013). *Status Update: Celebrity, publicity, and branding in the social media age*. Yale University Press.

Marwick, AE and boyd, d (2011). I tweet honestly, I tweet passionately: Twitter users, context collapse, and the imagined audience. *New Media & Society*, 13(1), 114–133. https://doi.org/10.1177/1461444810365313

Nogara, G, Vollmer, T, Rizzi, R, *et al* (2022). The disinformation dozen: An exploratory analysis of Covid-19 disinformation proliferation on Twitter. In

Proceedings of the 14th ACM Web Science Conference, 2022, 348–358. https://doi.org/10.1145/3501247.3531573

Salter, M, Brand, BL, Robinson, M, *et al* (2025). Self-diagnosed cases of dissociative identity disorder on social media: Conceptualization, assessment, and treatment. *Harvard Review of Psychiatry*, 33(1), 41–48. https://doi.org/10.1097/HRP.0000000000000416

Chapter 9

Bruckmann, C (2025). The friendship recession: The lost art of connecting. Harvard Kennedy School, Harvard University. https://www.happiness.hks.harvard.edu/february-2025-issue/the-friendship-recession-the-lost-art-of-connecting/

Ellison, NB, Steinfield, C and Lampe, C (2007). The benefits of Facebook "friends": Social capital and college students' use of online social network sites. *Journal of Computer-Mediated Communication*, 12(4), 1143–1168. https://doi.org/10.1111/j.1083-6101.2007.00367.x

Holt-Lunstad, J (2024). Social connection as a critical factor for mental and physical health: Evidence, trends, challenges, and future implications. *World Psychiatry*, 23(3), 312–332. https://doi.org/10.1002/wps.21224

Murthy, VH (2025). *My Parting Prescription for America*. Office of the U.S. Surgeon General. https://www.vivekmurthy.com/_files/ugd/9322fa_6d33185c1dab47ffa16f238f35b3b537.pdf

Putnam, RD (2000). *Bowling Alone: The collapse and revival of American community*. Touchstone Books/Simon & Schuster.

Chapter 10

Hoffner, CA and Bond, BJ (2022). Parasocial relationships, social media, & well-being. *Current Opinion in Psychology*, 2022 45, 101306. https://doi.org/10.1016/j.copsyc.2022.101306

Horton, D and Wohl, RR (1956). Mass communication and para-social interaction: Observations on intimacy at a distance. *Psychiatry*, 19(3), 215–229. https://doi.org/10.1080/00332747.1956.11023049

Lotun, S, Lamarche, VM, Matran-Fernandez, A and Sandstrom, GM (2024). *People perceive parasocial relationships to be effective at fulfilling emotional needs. Scientific Reports,* 14, 8185. https://doi.org/10.1038/s41598-024-58069-9

Chapter 11

Gass, RH (2015). Social Influence, Sociology of. In *International Encyclopedia of the Social & Behavioral Sciences* (Second Edition). Elsevier, pp. 348–354. https://doi.org/10.1016/B978-0-08-097086-8.32074-8.

Guéguen, N and Pichot, N (2001). The influence of status on pedestrians' failure to observe a road-safety rule. *The Journal of Social Psychology,* 141(3), 413–415. https://doi.org/10.1080/00224540109600562

Kahneman, D (2011). *Thinking, Fast and Slow.* Farrar, Straus and Giroux.

Chapter 12

Huta, V and Ryan, RM (2010). Pursuing pleasure or virtue: The differential and overlapping well-being benefits of hedonic and eudaimonic motives. *Journal of Happiness Studies,* 11, 735–762. https://doi.org/10.1007/s10902-009-9171-4

Kashdan, TB, Biswas-Diener, R and King, LA (2008). Reconsidering happiness: The costs of distinguishing between hedonics and eudaimonia. *The Journal of Positive Psychology,* 3(4), 219–233. https://doi.org/10.1080/17439760802303044

Kross, E, Verduyn, P, Demiralp, E, *et al* (2013). Facebook use predicts declines in subjective well-being in young adults. *PLOS ONE,* 8(8), e69841. https://doi.org/10.1371/journal.pone.0069841

Steger, MF, Kashdan, TB and Oishi, S (2008). Being good by doing good: Daily eudaimonic activity and well-being. *Journal of Research in Personality,* 42(1), 22–42. https://doi.org/10.1016/j.jrp.2007.03.004

Chapter 13

Deci, EL and Ryan, RM (2000). The "what" and "why" of goal pursuits: Human needs and the self-determination of behavior. *Psychological Inquiry,* 11(4), 227–268. https://doi.org/10.1207/S15327965PLI1104_01

Kashdan, TB and Rottenberg, J (2010). Psychological flexibility as a fundamental aspect of health. *Clinical Psychology Review,* 30(7), 865–878.

Ryan, RM and Deci, EL (2017). *Self-Determination Theory: Basic psychological needs in motivation, development, and wellness.* Guilford Press.

Chapter 14

Patrick, WL (2018). How your cell phone habits impact your productivity. *Psychology Today*.

Chapter 15

Clear, J (2018). *Atomic Habits: An easy and proven way to build good habits and break bad ones*. Avery.

Ganschow, B, Zebel, S, van Gelder, JL and Cornet, LJM (2024). Feeling connected but dissimilar to one's future self reduces the intention–behavior gap. *PLOS ONE,* 19(7), e0305815. https://doi.org/10.1371/journal.pone.0305815

Hershfield, HE, Goldstein, DG, Sharpe, WF, *et al* (2011). Increasing saving behavior through age-progressed renderings of the future self. *Journal of Marketing Research,* 48(SPL), S23–S37. https://doi.org/10.1509/jmkr.48.SPL.S23